Richard Lee Ummel, Sr.
August 1925-September 1981

Called According to His Purpose

***

From Indiana Farm-Life

to

Church Planting

on

Brazil's Coffee Frontiers

By
Richard L. Ummel

Edited & Prepared for Publishing By
Josephine (Ummel) Overhulser

Dedicated

to

Our Dear Children

Rick, Ted, Anita, Michael
and
Their Spouses

and to
Our Precious Grandchildren

Rachel, Ryan
Phillip, Tracy Lynn
Ricardo, Miguel, Michelle
Alexis, Jeremy, Madelyn Joy

and
Great Granddaughter

Victoria

May these memories be a blessing to you
and
to all who read these pages;

&

May you experience the reality
of
our Great God of love and faithfulness.

Preface

There is a story behind every book, they say: it's the way a book comes into being. This book is no exception. It has a story, and (we believe) a story in God's timing.

Believing that God had a *Plan* for his life, and a *Purpose* for every situation he faced, Richard "Dick" Ummel felt within himself an urgency to record experiences in his heritage and family as well as some of his experiences on the Frontiers of Brazil.

He wrote at a time in his life when he felt *God had slowed him down—perhaps for the Purpose* of writing this story—148 legal-sized pages; double spaced, typed on an old manual typewriter that could have benefited from some adjustments. These pages of his writings displayed a few insertions, deletions, and corrections.

At a point of time after Dick's death, this raw unpublished manuscript went to a friend of the family who graciously made copies to be distributed as a keepsake to the Ummel's four children in memory of the life and mission work of their father, and of their lives together as a family.

It's unknown how a copy of this manuscript found its way into the home of Dick's next younger brother, Eldon, who found it early in the Spring of 2006 among a large stack of old newspaper clippings. Eldon contacted his nephew—Dick's son. Ted knew of his father's manuscript and had a copy in his possession. With Ted's permission, Eldon made additional copies for his siblings—and no one else.

While attending a domino party at the home of Dick's youngest sister, this writer (a first cousin: our fathers were brothers) became aware of the manuscript. Sworn to secrecy on the existence of the document, she remained silent but kept thinking, *How can I beg, borrow, ste..., or somehow get a hold of a manuscript just to read...?"*

That evening I phoned cousin Eldon who said: "Oh, I think we can arrange that..." At the time he was in the process of making additional copies of the manuscript for the siblings who as yet hadn't received their copy.

I began reading and couldn't lay it down: "Whatever happens to this manuscript, a copy *must* get into the Historical Archives," I told Eldon, and offered to do the organizing and editing required to put it into book form for publishing. But permission to proceed had to come from sister-in-law, Jackie, who resided in Brazil.

After a few telephone calls, permission was granted; pictures began accumulating; and the project took shape. Much care has been taken to insert and delete according to the notes of the author, and retain his voice throughout the book. All dates, times, places, situations, and experiences have been verified by the family (and friends) as best they can remember or have recorded the events.

In the mid-1960's my husband and I with our two youngest sons, Jim and Dave, personally visited the Ummel family in Brazil. While editing this manuscript I've been blessed as I recalled fond memories of that trip, and our experiences in the villages.

Now—may you enjoy Dick's story told in his own words and recorded ... *for this Purpose.*

Josephine Marie (Ummel) Overhulser
Author & Editor

Table of Contents

INTRODUCTION

As he tells you in this record of his Memoirs, Richard Ummel had to "slow down" after being in the hospital for more than two weeks. During that time *Dick* felt led of God to write some of the facts—excerpts—of his early life on the farm, and then events that led him into our ministry and mission work in Brazil, South America.

Richard L. Ummel was a missionary—1956 to 1978—with the United Missionary Society (UMS) under the Missionary Church denomination. After our deputation work (1978), we asked for a *Leave of Absence* to enable us to remain in the United States until our youngest son completed his High School studies.

Several months later—the fall of 1978—Dick became seriously ill with congestive heart failure. During his recuperation he had time at home alone to work on his writing: I was working at the time to supplement our income. Many months later—after a partial recovery—Dick worked part time for our friend, Bob Wisler; then for a time with his brother, Herbert Ummel, as a "cow tester". Dick seemed to be doing better, and was greatly involved in Bible study groups—his passion.

Very unexpectedly, he suffered a stroke in the summer of 1981. It came as a great shock. However, he progressed steadily, felt much better, and all seemed well.

The evening of September 8, 1981—just three weeks and three days after his 56th birthday—we were visiting our dear friends, Dan and Gloria King. Dick and Dan had been discussing a portion of scripture. Later, while we were praying together *suddenly the Lord called Dick home.*

During our prayer time I felt the Presence of the Lord so near, and I was waiting to ask him if he had that feeling also. I would say that he did—for the Lord was taking Dick home to be with Him.

Although we knew Dick was not completely well, a person never expects death at such an early age. It was a shocking and devastating experience for me, and for our children.

At that time, our oldest son Rick, his wife Vikki and their daughter Rachel, were living in Minneapolis, Minnesota; our second son Ted, his wife Brenda and their son Phillip, were living in Argos, Indiana (two months later their daughter, Tracy, was born); our daughter, Anita, was in Puerto Rico doing her internship with Bethany Fellowship; and our youngest son, Michael, had just started his second year at Bethel College, Mishawaka, Indiana.

The same God who called a young couple to missionary service many years ago, is still the same today—*Jesus Christ is the same Yesterday, Today, and Forever*: Hebrews 13:8. It is only through His sustaining grace and love, and the knowledge of His Presence that any of us had courage to go on. God has surely been faithful and true to His Word—Praise His Name.

Jacquelyn "Jackie" Elizabeth (McReynolds) Ummel

Top Row: Michael, Anita, Ted, Rick
Seated: Dick, Jackie, Brenda w/Phillip, Vikki w/Rachel

Chapter 1

Clay in the Potter's Hands

Coronary Care Unit! ... Where are they taking me? ... I only came
for a check-up ... The nurse had said "only a couple of days for
observation."

B ecause I didn't feel well and had difficulty breathing, Dr. Abel,
our family doctor, had asked Jackie to take me to the Emergency
Room at Elkhart General Hospital (Elkhart, Indiana) to find out why
I was so completely exhausted: Congestive heart failure.

During the 16 days in the hospital—5 days in intensive care and
11 days in the ward—my body responded well to all the treatments
and medications. I felt much stronger, and had plenty of time for
meditation, prayer, and Bible study.

Each morning from 7:00 until 12:00 noon, the TV was tuned
to WHME Channel 46 from South Bend. I heard PTL, 700 Club,
and the religious services of Rev. Sumrall. Many times I went
back to sleep during the programs, yet sensed God's Presence so
near. Although too tired to read much, spiritual nurture came as the
doctors and nurses helped me physically.

Romans 8:29 reads: "We know that in all things God works for
the good of those who love Him, who have been *Called according to*
His purpose" (NIV, Emphasis mine). As a minister-missionary I had
often counseled others with this verse and many other passages from
the Bible, including: "I have learned the secret of being content in
any and every situation" (Philippians 4:11). *How can I honestly say*
that? Now the doctor told me that I must take three to four months
rest with very limited activity.

Always active, some people almost would have called me a "workaholic": I always felt better when active. If a job needed to be done, you would find me in the center of the activity. In organizing and supervising the construction of churches and parsonages on the mission field in Brazil, I always was ready and willing to do any part of any job. Many times I returned home as dirty and sweaty as any one of the laborers. On these occasions I became much closer to the men of the church. However, even with this type of extra work load, I did not neglect the spiritual ministry of teaching and preaching.

But today I was told—by my heart specialist—that I must stop all work. *How can I praise God for this situation and accept personally all of His promises?*

In answer, God very clearly showed me that He had another task for me—write a book—record the story of God's faithfulness and blessings. Although illness slowed me down at age 53, I had seen a lot accomplished during those years: running in high gear, doing several jobs at a time. Perhaps God used this way of slowing me down to do a different kind of work.

Through the pages of this book I hope to reveal some spiritual truths. Very few are original, but God helped me to apply them in my own way under His inspiration. In our modern culture of today, many values and goals are all mixed up. We look too much for man's approval rather than God's approval. God loves each one of us and has a dynamic responsibility for each one—not just the leaders. It is not the General that wins the battle, but the cooperation of every one under his command including the many foot soldiers.

Something is drastically wrong with any country that claims to have half of its population as church members, or Christians, and yet has so much sin and immorality. It's a sign of something very abnormal. Churches are using all kinds of programs, etc., and they are not holding their own. *Could this really be God's will or plan? What is God's will?*

I have had a great respect for our church leaders and pastors— always. Yet in 1947 I attended a church meeting in regards to the merger of our denomination with another denomination that we had been in association with for many years. It greatly shocked me to see some pastors stand up and state how God had revealed His will to them, and yet each had an entirely different opinion. Surely one of them didn't have God's guidance. *How can we know God's will when even our leaders don't always agree?*

I've seen instances where the majority vote *was not* God's will. Therefore I have prayed and meditated greatly seeking His will for my own life, and I am sure you have done the same for your life.

The democratic system is far from the theocratic system God originally planned and ordained for His chosen people. A qualified man for the position of president needs much training and preparation. Then many of his decisions are based on the poll rating of the common man rather than allowing him to seek God's plan along with his qualifying ability to make decisions. Then, should he not be re-elected, his opinions are almost completely disregarded. This is true in our country's government as well as the organization of the church.

In no way do I have the answers to all of these questions, but God does—we must seek Him: His values are different than ours. We have met church groups in Latin America that do not make a decision until they have 100% agreement in the decision making body. They fast and pray until God reveals His message. At times a majority vote would have been wrong.

Even with the assurance that God called me to missionary work, I couldn't understand why He chose me. I could teach my Sunday school class, but no person in the church had less ability in public speaking or singing. Yet, willingly, I wanted Him to use me. When returning home for our first furlough, I could show pictures and tell of God's blessing on our ministry in Brazil: God only needs a vessel through whom He can work, and that vessel need not be sensational. However, my conviction remained that if God had called someone with more talents, the results on the Field (in Brazil) would have been much greater. We soon learned that it isn't the abilities that count, but a genuine submission to do God's bidding—plus a compassion for souls.

Hopefully this book will help each reader to realize their responsibilities before God. We must re-evaluate our goals and priorities. We need leadership in the church, but the greatest need is more commitment on the part of each member of God's family. There must be more love between Christians—God is Love—no matter which church or denomination holds their membership. Many outstanding spiritual leaders have come into our home through TV and the radio. Most of them compliment each other, and it has been a privilege to hear and profit from them. In John 17 Christ prayed for unity and oneness among His followers. There is entirely too much competition between churches and their dynamic church leaders.

In Brazil I heard an excellent example of unity: *When we have mashed potatoes all of the peelings have been removed and they are blended together. This is how the Christians, through the spirit, should blend together to carry out His commission.*

My prayer is that as you read you will see the need in your everyday life to depend on God. Each person is important to Him. The greatest thing He wants is our willingness to be "Clay in the Potter's Hands."

Chapter 2

Jackie's Story

W hen you have had a lovely family of six children in 15 years, you feel you have done a big job. There is a certain amount of satisfaction and pride in each one of those children who ranged in age from 10-25 years. Yes, all seemed well—everyone was working hard. Even the father was away—sailing—trying to earn extra money to make sure all would be well in those difficult depression years. Soon the payments would be finished, and the farm located in Owen Sound, Ontario, Canada, would be theirs. Then the unbelievable happened. What would they do with another baby?

Well, they would make a way somehow. Without telling anyone about the little one she carried near her heart, Mother continued doing the farm work with the boys—summer hay and all. She took no medication, and was in poor condition for the ordeal she would go through on August 25, 1929—the day she gave birth to her baby. The tiny 4 pound girl named Jacquelyn Elizabeth—"Jackie" for short—became quite a novelty in the family and, at times, quite a nuisance for the big sisters who had to care for her when they preferred giving their attention to young gentlemen callers.

I am Jackie, the "after thought … mistake" or "an added blessing" who made her appearance that day in the home of Thomas Edward and Carolyn Amelia McReynolds. The year I was three and one-half, Daddy (age 58) lost the farm. From that time until I reached my 18th birthday, we lived in five different homes, and I attended five schools. Daddy had a hard time to keep the family going. An extra mouth to feed meant added responsibility. Life was difficult during those years.

We attended church regularly, and I knew Mother was a "born-again" loving Christian lady. Her whole life permeated God's love. Daddy—a good clean-living upright man—did not have a real "born-again" experience with God until in his 70's.

At age nine, we moved back to my daddy's birthplace—Vail's Point—the very house in which he had been born 64 years earlier. Here Daddy had fished as a boy with his two older brothers and his father. I enjoyed living and playing in the same setting in which my father had been raised. Living without electricity or inside plumbing was not unusual—we had never had such luxuries. Our water supply consisted of rain water caught in a cistern, and our drinking water came from a well one-half mile away from the house. We heated water either in a tea kettle or in the small reservoir at the back of our wood-burning stove. We took Saturday night baths in a big round tub placed by the kitchen stove for that purpose.

By the time I started school, my brother and I were the only children living at home. Being so much younger than my brothers and sisters, I was raised almost as an only child. My mother became my best friend and confidant—the dearest friend I could ever have had. I also greatly enjoyed being with Daddy; sitting on the end of a log as he sawed or chopped wood for our stove; sitting close by him as he mended fishing nets; and listening to the stories of his childhood. When he wasn't telling a story, Daddy whistled. You always knew where he was.

I spent much of my playtime in the sand and water at the shore of Georgian Bay. Summer holidays were highlights: nieces and nephews came to stay. What great times I had playing with other children near my age, and helping to care for the younger ones.

We lived a mile and a half from the school house. During my Public School days I had plenty of exercise walking a minimum of three miles per day. A neighbor girl lived fairly close. She and I walked those miles together. I enjoyed being with others of my own age: school was a pleasant experience.

In our small country school I was the only one in my class and studied at my own pace. After graduating from the eighth grade—age eleven—I started High School in the fall. We walked one mile to the bus, then rode sixteen miles to school, returned in late afternoon, and walked a mile home—my daily routine. But illness interrupted that school year, and High School began again for me at age thirteen.

During this year some young people my age who attended a Mennonite Brethren in Christ Church befriended me, and I began attending their meetings whenever possible. When the roads became impassable—drifted shut with snow—I stayed in town with my uncle, and attended every church service with them.

What a privilege the following summer to attend the Camp Meeting at Stayner, Ontario. What an experience: Rev. Q. J. Everest was the evangelist. I accepted Christ as my personal Savior. What a change: my loving and affectionate family had always given me a happy and secure feeling, but now I had "completeness" with Jesus in my life.

Upon graduation from Owen Sound Collegiate and Vocational Institute (OSCVI), I entered nurses' training at Kitchener-Waterloo Hospital in Kitchener, Ontario. Life was different living in a nurses' residence with so many girls of different backgrounds. It didn't take long to discover the many Christians among them, and during our three years of training, we made lifetime friendships. One year they elected me to serve as President of the Christian Nurses' Fellowship—all good preparation for my future work.

Only two weeks after entering hospital training, Mother had a severe cerebral hemorrhage. Some people suggested that I go home and care for her. But, thank God, others felt I should continue my studies to have "a profession". I continued my studies. After a year of needing care, Mother finally could manage the small apartment where she and Daddy lived.

During my third year of training we had three months of psychiatric training at the Ontario Hospital in London, Ontario. While there I attended a large Baptist church. During their Missionary Convention we heard Rev. Tommy Titcombe speak. God impressed His "Call" for missionary service on my life that night—never to this day have I doubted this Call.

Upon graduation from Kitchener-Waterloo Hospital in June 1950, I continued nursing and also took a semester of studies at Emmanuel Bible College, Kitchener, Ontario.

Then a miracle happened: the way opened up for me to visit Bethel College in Mishawaka, Indiana, U.S.A. I never thought that attending Bethel would be a possibility for me until I discovered I could work as College Nurse, and also work part-time in a local hospital to pay my way. In September (1951) I enrolled in a two-year Bible course, but told no one of my Call to missionary service.

My parents happily watched me study to prepare myself to better serve God, but I could tell they were disappointed that I wouldn't be working at home near them. Without a doubt they had qualms about a single girl going alone to a foreign country to do missionary work. All of this bothered me.

On campus I tried to reason with myself that I should stay near home; take care of my parents; earn lots of money; and send it to "missions"—thus make up for not going myself. For three months I felt miserable.

Finally in December 1951, unable to stand it any longer, I went forward at a special revival meeting on Campus. I promised the Lord that I would serve Him wherever He wanted me—regardless of parents, being single, or anything else. A sweet peace became mine by the end of that service, and my friends were amazed to hear of my Call to missionary work.

Another miracle happened a month later: a young football player, graduate of Manchester College, came to Bethel for more Bible courses. He had a missionary Call from years before, and also was preparing for foreign service work. Before long we both knew that God had brought us to the same school for a purpose—we became engaged in May, and in August 1952 we were married in my home church, Calvary Missionary Church, Owen Sound, Ontario, Canada.

My parents no longer needed to be concerned or worried about my service—God had sent a fine husband for their daughter. Happily they watched us prepare to serve God together in Brazil, South America.

Truly, our God moves in mysterious ways His wonders to perform, and *Calls us according to His purpose.*

Next, Richard tells his story: then after our marriage, our life and experiences are shared.

Chapter 3

Dick's Story

In the late 19th and early 20th century people knew the John Ummel family living in Harrison Township, Elkhart, Indiana, as a strong church family. In 1875 their parents, Joseph and Susannah Ummel, helped found the Bethel Missionary Church located seven miles south of Elkhart on County Road 7. At that time the church was known as the Bethel Mennonite Brethren in Christ Church. The denomination came from a Mennonite background influenced by the early Methodist circuit riders and evangelists.

The church influenced every part of the lives of the John Ummel, Sr., family. Regular devotions each day gave direction to each part of their home-life. Attendance at every church service and many home meetings became a vital part of their entire family: father, mother, and their ten children.

The first four children of John and Ella (Lambert) Ummel were boys. Two of these, Joseph (first) and Paul (third), went to Nigeria, West Africa, as pioneer missionaries. As time went on, each son and daughter became active in their own church where they moved after their marriage.

Edward, the second son, was the first child of the family to be married. Upon his marriage to Edith Anglemyer, Edward rented his uncle's farm just two miles away from the Ummel homestead in Harrison Township. Their first son, Robert Dale, was born January 24, 1924. A second son arrived August 15, 1925 — his name, Richard Lee. Being the first two grandchildren, these little boys received a great deal of attention and prayers.

Richard—that's me—a very active inquisitive little boy, wanted to know the "how" and "why" of everything that moved or made a noise, and he loved animals. From the moment he could crawl, he got into everything. If a chair sat close to the table or dresser, Richard would soon be on top of it. Toddling around the yard he saw everything, and soon noticed the newborn chicks. If his mother didn't see him, and come soon enough, he would love them to death by squeezing them.

One day Robert came screaming and crying into the house saying that a mother hen had jumped on him and picked him. Immediately mother came out to find Richard. He had a little stick and was chasing the mother hen across the yard. This same spirit of determination and perseverance continued throughout his life.

In those days the farmers used horses in farming. These big strong horses weighed nearly a ton each. Most farmers planned on a colt each year or so from every mare. A big strong well-broken mare wasn't always tame after she gave birth to a colt. When Richard was about two and one-half years old, our big mare had a colt. She didn't want anyone to enter the pasture where she and her colt were, and would chase and even try to kick or bite any intruder.

One morning Richard's mother saw her toddler on his way to see the new colt. She watched in helpless terror as the big mare stepped up between the colt and the little mischievous inquisitive toddler. Undaunted and fearless, Richard walked right under the big mare to see the colt a little better. Amazingly the big mare only looked at him and did not make any sign of hurting him. Satisfied that he had seen what he wanted to see, Richard ran back to the house when his mother called. This began a life full of many incidents of God's Hand clearly resting upon this young man in a protective and directive manner, guiding the life of Richard for His Own glory.

A few years later Edward purchased a 60-acre farm three miles east of Foraker, Indiana. Here Richard spent his boyhood days and began his schooling at the public school in New Paris, only a few miles away.

Every few years another brother or sister entered their home until they numbered ten children. Another child was never looked upon as a liability, but as a gift from God, and an asset to help with the work. In addition to this, God had ordained to parents—mothers and fathers—the responsibility of nurturing their children for spiritual service in His Kingdom. The children brought joy to their home.

A small stream, or creek, ran through the farm. With the chores done and the work finished, Richard and some of his brothers could be found swimming or fishing—we always took time for some recreation.

The big depression hit about the time Richard started school. Father had no extra spending money or allowance money for any of the children. However, almost all of the families in our area lived under similar financial circumstances. In fact, Richard does not remember his father having any extra cash on hand during those early school days.

Everyone helped. We boys always went out with our father as he did the chores. Each of us had our own responsibility of work, and it varied in proportion to the ability, size, and age of each child.

In the morning before going to school, I milked one cow by hand, and again in the evening, and at each milking. My older brother milked two or three cows. Gradually we each did more work and the younger ones started their chores also. As time went on I had many things to do such as the complete responsibility for feeding the chickens and pigs—knowing and measuring the exact quantities each needed per feeding. As the younger children became older, they helped me by getting hay down from the hay-mow, silage from the silo, straw for bedding, and feeding the livestock—cattle, horses, sheep, pigs, and chickens.

Our clothes were plain, but sufficient. In the summer we only wore shoes on Sunday and to other weekday church services. When school started in the fall, each boy received two pair of blue-jeans and a pair of shoes. During the winter, patches became necessary for our clothes—especially over the knees. By spring mother cut off our pants at the knees and they were ready for summer wear. As the days grew colder we each had sweaters and jackets to wear—usually hand-me-downs from older children at church.

Mother worked hard, too. She always had a big garden, and another space of more than an acre that we called a truck patch. Here we planted sweet corn, pop corn, vegetables, strawberries, raspberries, and more. By fall her jars of canned fruits and vegetables, the bags of potatoes, and a barrel or so of apples, completely filled our small cellar. We gathered all the fallen apples to make sweet cider, vinegar, and apple butter.

Each year father took about five bushels of wheat to a mill to be ground into flour: mother baked us home-made bread. As father husked corn by hand, he selected the best ears to be set aside as seed for the next year, and some to be ground into cornmeal to make cornbread and mush.

About the only things we purchased from the grocery store were sugar, salt, spices, and a few other items. For these necessities, mother traded eggs. We were almost self-sufficient from our land.

We never went hungry. Many evenings we had only apple butter on bread. I even preferred dipping this into my glass of milk instead of having it separately. After having mush (made from cooked corn-meal) for supper, mother placed the left-over portion in a pan. By morning it had become firm. She sliced it, fried it in a skillet, and served it with syrup on top for breakfast the next morning. We never knew of the suffering that many children in the cities went through during those depression years.

Sunday evenings we usually had popcorn. If we were still hungry we could pour milk and sprinkle sugar over the popcorn in our bowl.

Mother usually washed our clothes on Monday. She used a big boiler on top of the kitchen range to heat the wash water. So on washday she always had a big pot of beans beside the boiler with a couple pieces of pork in it. This usually lasted for both meals that day.

Farm produce prices came to an all-time low. So a neighbor helped my father butcher our hogs and we peddled the meat in Elkhart (Indiana). In this way we earned some money for taxes and farm payments. The hams and shoulders were the hardest to sell: they cost more, and the people could not afford them. Mother sugar-cured these unsold hams and kept them for our home use. We may not have had a great variety of food on the table, but it satisfied our hunger, and we ate well.

I can remember one time when several of the children needed work done on their teeth. With no cash available, the dentist gladly accepted several hams as payment.

We always enjoyed the out-of-doors, and we boys ran a trap line every fall. My older brother milked my cow, and I started out at dawn to cover about two miles and check two to three dozen traps. Eldon, my next younger brother, usually went with me on this early morning hike. In those days we caught more rabbits than anything else. That meant we would have wild rabbit meat for supper. We did catch a few opossum, skunks, muskrats, and later on, mink. We three boys then divided the cash between us. If we received a few dollars for these furs, we used it to buy our own shoes and sweaters. In the long run our recreation helped the family budget, and we also learned to care for our shoes and clothes better: we learned their value.

In addition to the stream that crossed our pasture, we had a small marsh on the farm. We spent much time there and caught three or four snapping turtles each year. Some of their shells measured more than a foot across. We could sell them for $.50 to $.75 each. Consequently, we boys were always on the lookout for these turtles. We could catch them easily when they crawled across the pasture. But in the mud at the bottom of the creek, it was much harder, and very difficult to know which end was the head. So we planned an attack on the big turtles: I put my hands on top of the shell and pushed him down so he couldn't swim away. Immediately the turtle's head would come out. Then Eldon grabbed it by its tail and threw it up on the bank. As far as I can remember, money from trapping and hunting turtles became our only personal cash during the early 1930s.

Nobody in the rural areas had electricity at that time. We had two or three kerosene lamps in the house and a simple lantern to carry around to do the chores. By the time I reached the third grade of school, father purchased an Aladdin lamp. This helped by giving more light for reading and doing our homework. Very seldom I brought school books home because after the chores and eating supper, I was tired—ready for bed.

A tall black wood-burning stove sat in the middle of our living room. The chimney pipe went through our upstairs bedroom, and took some chill off the room in the wintertime. A big range stove sat in the kitchen. We used it year-round for cooking, and it kept the kitchen toasty-warm in the winter.

By the time I was eight years old, father took us boys along to the woods to cut firewood. We boys took turns on one end of the two-man crosscut saw. About every ten minutes we traded "turns" on the saw. When the weather became too cold for us, father made a bonfire with the top limbs of the trees. While cutting down trees, only the one who helped on the crosscut saw was allowed close to the tree. We cut only the dead or hollow trees. We never cut the solid trees that could be sold for lumber, and the trees always seemed to fall where father said they would fall.

We had the luxury of running water in our home—when we pumped the handle—ha! Many of our neighbors had to go outside to get their water. Our pump and sink sat in a small cloak room just off the kitchen. We passed through this room on our way in and out of the house. Here we could wash up as we entered the house—hands, face, and even our feet often needed this attention.

We each had responsibilities in the house, too. If given a choice, I always went out—one way or another—to help father rather than wash or wipe dishes. I never did get to do my share of work in the house.

Cutting and shocking grain is a big job for every farm family. It ripened during the hottest days of the summer. My father used our three big horses to pull the grain binder, and we boys always helped shock the bundles.

One day in 1935—I was ten—father cut about 10 acres of wheat. We boys had most of the cows milked by the time he brought home the team of sweating horses. After we finished the chores and ate our supper, we went back to shock the bundles of wheat. It must have been close to full moon as we could see very well in the moonlight. About 2:30 a.m. we finished shocking all of the wheat that father had cut. We boys could put as many bundles in the shocks as our father. Much later I learned that we had Beardy Wheat, and if this work had been done in the daytime, the sharp points in the head of each stem would actually penetrate the skin of your hands. I thought my father did it in order to save a day's work. Early the next day we had our milking done, and father was out there to finish cutting the field of wheat.

Threshing the grain and filling the silo took a big crew. All the neighbors worked together, exchanging labor and helping one another during this time of the year. We enjoyed those days with all the excitement of helpers and big machinery—so interesting to watch the big steam engine come down the road and be belted up to the thresher. The owner of the big rig also had a strong team of horses hitched to a wagon to carry water and supplies. About six or eight teams of horses and wagons were needed along with four to six men to pitch up the bundles. Our job was to carry fresh water to the workers.

The ladies also worked hard to prepare the noon meal. While the men ate, we boys liked to walk around outside and look at all the big horses feeding on their hay. After the men ate, we children sat down at the table with the ladies. It would take from two to four weeks for this crew to thresh out the wheat and oats of the whole neighborhood.

Generally father used all three of our big horses when he plowed with the riding plow. But many times he would use the walking plow to do the garden and truck patch, and I followed in his shadow—trying to walk in his tracks. Usually I took two steps to each one of his. In a short time of following the plow, I'd have plenty of earthworms for bait. When I became tired of following, I went back to the creek to fish.

Father also farmed two other small farms on shares. The back corner of our farm touched the back corner of one of these fields that father farmed—both fields lay in the same section. So by walking through the fields and climbing over the fences, it wasn't far from our house to where father worked. Many evenings father had me come and meet him in those fields. After he had unhitched the horses from the plow or harrow, he would lift me up on one of the big horses. Then I would ride and drive the horses home around by the road while father walked the shortcut taking the cows from the pasture to the barn for milking. By the time I arrived with the horses, he already had several cows milked.

Bringing home the horses from the back field began at about age four or five—before I was old enough to milk. Sometimes my younger brother, Eldon, went along. We were a rather small pair to be riding such huge horses, but father trusted us and knew we would hang on. After a long day of work the horses were tired, and walked home with no danger of taking off on a run.

The Ummel name has been associated with registered Holstein cows for many years. My father got started in dairy farming while still in his teens at his father's home, and always was interested in improving our dairy herd.

During the depression years father bought a good herd-sired male calf only a few months old. He had to get a loan from the local bank—it was hard times—but it paid off eventually when we had one of the top herds of the county.

By 1936 Holsteins filled our little barn completely with some heifers in box pens in one end of the chicken house, and calves in the old hog house. That winter we had nine milk cows and eight heifers ready to freshen (give birth, and milk). We knew that we couldn't continue on that small farm.

In the fall of 1936 my father rented a larger 220 acre dairy farm about three miles southeast of Benton, Indiana. The big barn had 36 stanchions (milking stalls). We moved the cattle in the fall of that year in order to house the dairy herd. Soon we were milking 17 cows and had enough heifers and calves to fill almost every stanchion.

Three big sows remained on the small farm. So when we moved, father kept four of our gilts (small pigs). Before long, all of the box stalls were filled. Many of our neighbors and relatives wondered how my father could have had so much livestock on the 60 acre farm.

Father purchased a 32 volt Delco generator and light plant. This greatly helped our operation. If there wasn't enough wind for the windmill to pump water for the house and dairy barn setup, we simply turned on the electric motor and pumped plenty of water. Also, now we could have a motor on our cream separator that we previously had turned by hand: we sold the cream—all the skim milk went to the hogs.

The winter of 1936-1937 my chores consisted of milking three or four cows by hand—morning and evening—and throw down the hay, straw, and silage. In the evenings we helped father in the barn until everything was finished. Every morning we were up at 5:30 in order to milk our cows before the school bus came.

Unfortunately the farm sold out from under us a year later, and father had to find another farm to rent. At this time one of the largest farms in the county became available for rent—260 acres with a big set of farm buildings—located several miles east of Elkhart on the Middlebury Road (County Road 14). This setup accommodated both dairy and hogs. We now had about 12 sows, and fattened about 90 pigs twice a year. Our dairy herd had 20 to 24 milk cows besides all of the young stock. We "vealed" all the bull calves and raised the females. This farm seemed ideal for our situation.

Because the R.E.M.C. Electric Company had plans to connect the farm to their electrical system, the buildings had been wired: we hooked up our generator plant and had electrical power in advance of the surrounding farms. At times the plant broke down, and we reverted back to kerosene lights. But we now had added a Coleman gas lantern for such an emergency. Many times we used this lantern for light while doing the chores.

This 260 acre farm needed a tractor. In the spring father made the best deal on a Silver King tractor. The next year he traded it for a W.C. Allis Chalmers tractor. We also maintained four or five farm horses. We used the teams to haul manure, plant corn, and for the lighter farm work. Since we husked our corn by hand, the team made it much more practical in moving the wagon through the rows of cornstalks.

Each year we planted more than 100 acres of corn in addition to 40-50 acres of oats and soybeans. In those days we planted soybeans only for hay and not as a cash crop. Wheat was our only cash crop. All other crops became feed for the hogs and dairy cows.

Previously this farm had been run by at least two families—two houses stood on it. Our father and we four sons managed the farm excellently. Now age 13—a big strong lad—many times I took the tractor to the field at daybreak while my father and brothers milked the cows. After they finished the chores and breakfast, father took over the tractor. When the time came for evening chores, I again drove the tractor until dark. This gave me six to eight hours each day on the tractor.

Another big job: harvesting corn. Every Saturday or holiday during harvest time found us in the cornfield. Since the first four in our family were boys, we all went out to husk corn. The team pulled our farm wagon that had the grain bed and a big backboard on one side which kept the corn from being thrown completely across the wagon. We husked five rows at a time: father took the two outside rows, Robert took the next row, I took the second row from the wagon, and Eldon and Herbert had the first row, next to the wagon. Occasionally someone did get hit with an ear of corn. It hurt.

We took two big wagons to the field and filled them both by noon, and filled them again by evening. During the week days, father husked about an acre a day by himself. We usually finished with the corn harvest during Thanksgiving vacation. Because husking corn happened in the fall, we often took a jug of fresh apple cider along to the field to quench our thirst.

As we husked corn, we had long visits with our father. It was so good to all be together. He wanted to know about our school work and what we were learning in our agriculture classes. He spoke often of his childhood, and we loved to listen to his stories.

In 1941 our three-year lease terminated with the owner of the farm. Our parents decided to buy a farm of our own. We had a Registered Holstein Cattle Dispersal Sale. Father had the herd on "test" and had a pedigree for each cow. It turned out to be one of the best Holstein sales of the year in northern Indiana. Some cows went to out-of-state buyers. At that time the cattle owners could also bid at a dispersal sale. Father bought back some of the better cows for us to start over again.

Because many doctors and lawyers were investing in the area around Elkhart, farm land a little distance from Elkhart and Goshen sold for much less money. We bought a farm in Franklin Township located in the southwest corner of Kosciusko County—our address: R.R. #1, Claypool, Indiana.

At age 15, I weighed 175 pounds—only a little less than my father. Everything looked good: our dairy herd had become one of the best in that county: our family won and earned many blue ribbons at the 4-H Fairs and the district Holstein-Friesian cattle shows.

Then father became ill. I should have known that it was serious when he began going regularly to the doctor. He had Undulant Fever and it had weakened his heart. In the fall of 1941 and during that winter, we boys did all of the heavy work: some days he never left the house. We had a late spring in 1942.

In those days the rural schools usually let out by April 15, and we knew how to take care of the farm. Father did come out and plant the corn after we had everything ready. We even put the corn and fertilizer into the two-row corn planter for him.

We finished planting the corn June 15. That night we had fresh strawberry short-cake for supper. As we finished eating and sat visiting around the table as usual, father took one big gasp and leaned back in his chair. We immediately carried him to the living room couch.

They sent *me* to get the doctor. Since we had no telephone system on our road, I drove the car to Black's Country Store, one and one-half miles west of our place. Some one in the store phoned for a doctor. On the way back home I became so anxious to get home that as I went around a curve, the loose gravel caused my car to slip off the road and into the ditch. I jumped out and ran the rest of the way home—only about one-half mile. I reached home before any of the neighbors or the doctor arrived.

The doctor said it was "a heart attack," and father had died before we had laid him down on the couch. This was a terrible shock to all of us, leaving us stunned with grief—a mother and her family of nine children: Robert 18½; Richard (me), almost 17; Eldon, 15 on the day of the funeral; Herbert, 13 next month; Carol, 11; Joan, 9; Lois, 7; Stanley, 5; Max would be 2 in about 6 weeks; and our poor dear mother expecting her 10th child in another four or five weeks.

Edward Ummel—August 1898-June 1942

We were a sad, lost little bunch, but the farm work had to be done and the cattle cared for. We dug in and worked together. On July 18 (1942) our little sister, Phyllis, arrived. It never entered our minds to separate the family, or ask for welfare.

Only the initial down payment and the first payment had been made on our farm. God helped us, and we were able to manage. How thankful we were for our own farm: no one would have consented renting—much less selling—a dairy farm to a woman and a bunch of boys.

Since I had grown up in such a close relationship to my father, it was only my strong faith in God that carried me through those days and weeks. I took more interest than ever in spiritual things. I asked

God what to do in many of the most simple, or difficult, decisions. I appreciated more than ever the Christian nurture and influence of a Christian home, and the teachings my father had given me.

Father had been an industrious man and a good manager. In the days when we sold only the cream, he began raising pigs: feeding the pigs the skimmed milk was really using the milk to an advantage. I remember as a young boy I often carried the lantern for father as we finished the chores, and feeding the pigs after separating the milk was the last chore to be done. I enjoyed being with him every possible moment: he's my father.

The spring before father's death we had about 60 young pigs—almost the same in size and age—just about the best we ever had. Then only a few days after father's death many men came along trying to buy the pigs. Some of these hog buyers actually offered us only about half the value of weaning pigs sold at the local market. Of course, we did not sell them.

I could tell you of many other stories how business men—and others—tried to take advantage of our widowed mother: unbelievable! However most of the Holstein breeders in the area who knew our family well enough, knew we would be continuing the dairy business: they respected our family.

I took charge of feeding these shoats (young, weaned pigs), and they got along very well. We marketed our hogs at about 220 lbs. each. I tried to watch the daily market and sold them according to the market price. A local trucking firm contracted with us to haul them to the stockyards in Warsaw. Having gone there in earlier years with my father, I knew where father sold them. As the pigs were weighed and their value figured out, the buyer asked, "Whose name should I put on this check?"

Although a big fellow, I was only 17—a minor—but replied that "the check has to be in my name because there are bills for me to pay here in Warsaw; the local feed dealer is awaiting payment; and at this time my mother is in the Rochester Hospital having just had a gall bladder operation."

The dealer replied that he "could not possibly make out a check of this size to a minor child."

The truck driver then stepped up and told the buyer that he knew me, and I was doing a man's job on the farm since my father's death: if anything went wrong with the money, he personally would be responsible.

My name went on the check, and the banker accepted the check without any question, treating me as an adult. From a part of the deposit I paid our outstanding bills and took care of mother's hospital bill. Of necessity I had to grow up fast. At that time, the responsibility of keeping our home and family together became the most important thing in my life.

Church held more importance to me than worldly entertainment. Some may have called me a "loner", but with close fellowship with God, I didn't care what the other youth said or did. My father wished to raise his family as he had been raised. Church and religious meetings had been the most important events for both of my parents. I never knew what it was like not to be in the church services—not only Sunday school and church on Sunday mornings, but Sunday night and any time the church had a service our entire family was present.

I had a great interest in listening to my two uncles, Joseph and Paul, as they told of their pioneer missionary experiences in Northern Nigeria, West Africa. They had furloughs home only every three years or so. I even wrote a few letters to them while they lived in Nigeria.

One Sunday morning our car broke down. Rather than miss Sunday school and church, I took my little brother with me on the bicycle to church—about seven miles one way. Several times in my youth I went forward for prayer. Then when we moved to our own farm, the local Christian Church at Palestine (Indiana) paid my way to a youth camp at Winona Lake. My life changed that summer of 1941, for I accepted Christ as my Savior. God really changed my whole life.

The spirit of God spoke to me in the morning service without even an altar call. I laid my head on the arm of my chair and began weeping and praying. As everyone left for the noon meal, a pastor-counselor came back and prayed with me. God revealed to me that my cow had been my god. She (the cow) had remained unbeaten in the show ring. As a calf we won the blue ribbon at the northern Indiana Black-and-White Show from a class of about 20 other calves. I could even call her in the pasture and she would come to me. So when I accepted Christ and put Him in first place, everything became different.

As I walked across the beautiful conference grounds at Winona Lake that day, it appeared as though every tree lifted up its limbs as arms to praise God. I hadn't gotten into deep sin, but nobody needs to go into the depth of sin to be saved. All need salvation. From the outside I looked fine: always in church. But now I knew the personal relationship with God. What a difference in my heart!

Shortly after my conversion experience we visited the Church of God at Akron, Indiana. They welcomed us as though we had always been among them. Of course a large family of nine children doesn't come into a church unnoticed. I became very active in the youth services. Within a few months they asked me to teach a Sunday school class, and I always took my smaller brother and sister along. We had a radio in the barn, and kept in contact with the Missionary Church through *Your Worship Hour* by Rev. Q. J. Everest who had been our pastor at the Zion Missionary Church in Elkhart, Indiana.

Our normal hour for milking in the morning remained the same on Sundays. So we finished, got ready, and left on time for church services. Our big car became one of the first cars in the church parking lot every Sunday morning.

On Sunday evening we milked our cows more than an hour early because we wanted to get to church in time for the Youth Meeting which began one hour earlier than the evening service. Getting to church never presented a problem because we never thought of working in the fields on Sunday.

Only a rare occasion prevented us from attending the mid-week prayer service and Bible study. After my *born-again* experience, my innermost desire was to be in God's house for spiritual nurture.

Previous to conversion I went along because father demanded this in our household: it was the way of our family. My love and respect for father prevented me from displeasing him. Never in my life could I understand why some children wanted to run away from home. However, at times I did question some ways he had in farming.

My studies in agriculture interested me, and Purdue University had an outstanding experimental station. At school we had access to their (PU) recommendations. Father said that "whenever a better way presented itself, we should consider changing our way. But we can't do every new idea until proven in our area."

Therefore when my father told me to do farming his way, there was no question. As far as I can remember, I never talked back to my father.

Many denominations influenced my spiritual nurturing. If there was not a service in our home church, we went to revivals or special meetings of other churches in our area. During the summer we attended many services at the Winona Lake Conference Grounds only 16 miles from our farm. Especially after father's death, I took more interest in these meetings. Many times they had missionary pictures and challenges after the evening service. When rain or other weather conditions kept farmers out of the fields, I went to the services at Winona regardless of the Conference in session. Usually my mother and some of my brothers and sisters went along. But many times I went alone.

After father was "called home", God took my father's place in my life. In addition to my regular devotions, I asked Him for help and guidance in every minute detail of my life.

Our farm program continued in much the same way as when father was with us. We had worked closely with him and knew how to manage the farm—even the details of crop rotation in each field.

My older brother, Robert, had helped mother in the house much more than I, and he also had more experience in the dairy barn. Since I had worked with the tractor while they milked the cows, it was only natural for Robert to be more in charge of the dairy barn while I supervised the outside work. But we all worked together as a family unit.

Father had depended heavily upon me to keep the machinery repaired. If an implement broke down or the plow shares needed changing, usually I did it. When I was nine years old a big hay rope broke while we were putting the hay in the barn. Father called a neighbor to splice it together. I watched every move he made. That night I took a small rope and showed my father that I could splice a rope. After that, splicing the rope became my job. Upon watching father change a plow share, I changed the next one. Father trusted me with the farm machinery.

Sparrows made nests in the hay car at the extreme top of the hay mow. My brothers helped put the heavy wooden ladder up against the track where the car ran to take the slings of hay to the various lofts, and to the far end of the barn. Most of the time we couldn't knock the nest out without going up and taking it out by hand. Someone had to climb the ladder to do this. I asked God to protect me every step as I went up that big ladder. The track would sway back and forth a little, but I knew its strength—each sling of hay weighed 700–1000 lbs—but I still prayed all the way up and down the ladder.

Threshing time meant that many farmers worked together. I harnessed our team to haul the bundles of wheat. We had a strong team and I never worried about overloading the wagon with grain. In fact, I had earlier asked my father why we never took them to the annual horse-pulling contest at the county fair. Father said the team had never been trained to pull a dead weight to the maximum. Besides that, he loved the team too much to abuse them in a pulling contest.

Most of the other drivers were mature men, but I was not to be outdone in putting on a load of grain for the threshers. I challenged the men who pitched the bundles up to me to just try and cover me up. The faster they threw the bundles, the faster I put them in place. If they came too fast—sometimes by two men pitching—I just kicked them into the middle of the wagon and stamped them down in order to hold the outside bundles in place. When loaded, my load may not have looked as neat as the others but sometimes the threshing machine registered that I had almost twice as many bushels of grain as some of the wagons.

One time I had a big wagon load at the far end of the field. This farmer had only disked the grain field instead of plowing—it was rough. I prayed for the Lord to help me get the load to the threshing machine without upsetting it. I picked up the lines and snapped them lightly meaning to say, "Get up, there." Instead I said out loud, "Let's go, Jesus," in an attitude of prayer. Immediately the team started cautiously for the barn, and not a bundle shifted on the wagon. I surely praised God for every job he helped me do.

Many times we had to run our tractor around the clock to get our spring crops planted. We only stopped to refill the gas tank and check the oil. Then another one of us took a turn. One week the tractor only cooled off from 12:00 midnight Saturday until 12:00 Monday morning. By keeping the W.C. Allis Chalmers tractor on the continual move, we could have 10 acres a day plowed and worked into condition for planting. It had about 24 horse power on the draw bar and pulled a 14 inch two-bottomed plow. This way the team could plant the freshly plowed ground in corn every day.

Eldon, who grew up as my shadow, usually ran the tractor during the night hours; Robert took over during the day; and I drove between times to give them some breaks. Since father wasn't around to plant the corn, I drove the team and did the planting. When we remodeled our barn, we had no horse stable: we purchased another tractor. Then we did all the planting with the smaller tractor.

One teacher told me that it would be possible for me to finish high school by correspondence. So I asked God's guidance.

The state law demanded everyone had to attend school until 16 years of age. Sports were my interest in school—we boys loved softball and basketball. For several years no grass grew around the bases in our lower yard. Every spare moment we had a ball game going. Often the neighbor boys joined us four boys for regular softball games in our yard.

"The Lower Yard"
RR #1, Claypool, IN

The hay loft also had a basketball ring. Our coach gave old basketballs and nets to most boys that had a basketball hoop. We had to bring in the old net before he gave us a new one. There were times when our net was in shreds every three or four weeks. Since our high school had only 35 students, every boy was expected to go out for the team. Several neighbor boys came regularly to practice—the old barn saw a lot of action. Eldon had several spots where he could hit nine out of ten shots regularly. He played on our high school basketball team three years; I played on the first team both years that I attended Beaver Dame High School. As the years went by, all of the boys in our family made the team during their high school years.

Mr. (Roland) Ferverda, the principal of Beaver Dam H.S., took a personal interest in me. He came to see me near my 17th birthday, and promised me that if I kept up in my studies, I could finish my last year of high school at Beaver Dam. In September, I missed 11 of the 20 school days. Several times during the year I went ahead of the class in my studies by studying at home. The farm work came first, but God also helped me find time to study.

Even before father's death dairying soon became more and more the central interest on the farm. We tried to raise everything on the farm to not necessitate much buying, except for the supplements needed in a balanced dairy ration (feed). Loose housing in the barn for the dairy cows meant we needed a lot of straw for bedding—we ran short every year. Because straw cost nearly as much as hay, we made bedding from corn fodder. It took a lot more work, and many a very cold day found us bringing this fodder in from the fields with our team and wagon.

When we filled our two silos in the fall, we had eight men cutting the cornstalks by hand. Father had purchased a new John Deere corn binder when we lived on the farm east of Elkhart. With the binder, four men picked up the bundles faster than the eight men could cut and load a wagon. We used the binder to help our neighbors. Father also purchased our own used Papec silo filler, and we began to cut our corn fodder for bedding. This meant that the cornstalks had to be shocked, hauled to the barn, and run through the ensilage cutter. Many times the cows ate part of their bedding. This chopped fodder worked better than straw.

We began husking corn while there was still a lot of moisture in it, and then scattered the ears out in the big corn crib. By scattering it out, the corn dried without harm from mold or heat. After husking two to four rows around the field, I would cut the cornstalks with the binder. After we finished husking each field, we would shock the fodder. By cutting the stalks this early, the fodder still had food value. Many times we had 20 acres husked before any neighbor harvested the same acreage with their corn-picker. Each year we cut about 30-40 acres of cornstalks in this way to use for bedding.

We were constantly busy almost every day of the year—keeping everything fed while keeping our expenses down. All this extra work was **not** done by the ordinary farmer who went out and bought straw. But we had no money for straw, and made our way by using corn fodder instead of straw. We thanked God that at least we had our own farm to work and pay for. Renting would have been out of the question for a widow with a family of ten children.

During the first years after father's death, our cream and milk checks kept the farm going. When we sold our hogs, the money went on the mortgage. Later as our dairy herd increased, we stopped raising hogs and concentrated on the dairy.

All heifer calves we raised. Each year we sold from two to four of our dairy cows either in the county sale, or at the Regional Registered Holstein Consignment Sale. We sold only the cows that would be in their prime condition—ready to freshen (calve), or had just calved: they would bring the best prices. When the poorer or cull cows became unprofitable to keep, they sold for beef. Had we not spent money to modernize our dairy barn in order to sell "grade-A" milk, the note (mortgage) on the farm would have been liquidated much sooner.

World War II began December 7, 1941—about six months before our father's death. As we were growing up the local draft board listed us "2C—essential farm workers". Then in 1945 the draft board had to meet their quota.

They called mother, Robert and me, to appear before the board. They advised it would be necessary for one of us—either Robert or I—to enter the armed service. Robert felt he could in no way be in charge of keeping the entire farm operation going. So he was the one who volunteered himself to the draft board.

Easter 1945—Robert in Germany
Back: Eldon, Herb, Dick, Mother
Front: Carol, Joan w/Max, Lois w/Phyllis, Stanley & his pet

Then about a year later—April 1946—Eldon was drafted.

Note: *Eldon served in the army from April 1946 to June 1947. His term of service: six months. When his time ended, he agreed—upon the request of his Commanding Officer—to serve longer. He "only needed to get back in time for college." Eldon's 13-plus months of service exempted him from being recalled for duty in the Korean War. He remained at home to attend college and assist on the farm.*

Now, two of the four oldest brothers were serving in Europe: Eldon in Italy, and Robert in Germany. Our farming operations had to change. That summer we completely remodeled our barn. Uncle Richard Blessing—married to father's sister, Elizabeth—assisted us, especially with the cement work. We installed a Surge milking machine and built the new milk house. Now we could carry on our same operation with less help, and the setup qualified us to sell "grade-A" milk.

Father had seen the potential of this—had been dreaming of this—from the time he first saw the big barn. He had discussed things like this with us, and we were fulfilling his dream with this dairy barn arrangement. We now had one of the nicest dairy barns in the county. Even with my good clothes on after the Sunday evening service, I could go into the barn and throw hay into the cow mangers without getting dirty.

Making hay has always been a big job on any dairy farm. Only when all of our farm work got caught up were we free to help other neighboring farmers—thus earn a little personal spending money.

In the spring of 1947 my brother Eldon who had just returned from the army, and I bought a used Case hay baler. They manufactured very little farm machinery during the war—new ones were unavailable and for this one, we paid more than the price of a new baler. He and I worked out a deal with mother: we would bale all the hay on our farm, if we could use the tractor to do custom baling for other farmers.

We went all over the neighborhood with the baler. We worked as late as the hay stayed dry enough to bale—some nights, after dark. The baler handled a lot of hay, but required four people to do the operation. We usually had someone to ride the baler and help feed the hay in order to handle as much hay as possible in the shortest time. We hired our younger brothers and sisters, paying them the going rate of an adult because they were doing the job of an adult. Joan, my sister about 15 years old, became one of the best drivers we could have had. Almost always we pulled a wagon, and the farmer whose hay we were baling did his own loading.

During those days I was in top physical condition, and could pick up a bale from the ground and throw it up on top of the wagon. That first year we baled more than 30,000 bales. The Lord gave us good weather when we cut it, and we had our own baler to harvest it. Many of the farmers waited until their hay was well ripened. We cut early to be ready to bale for those neighbors, and yet filled our barn with the best of hay.

I loved farming. Agriculture had been my major in high school. Through the farm magazines we kept up with the latest in dairy farming. My dream: to own one of the finest registered Holstein herds in the state. I was well on the way, even though officially the herd belonged to my mother.

Although I enjoyed farming and it took up most of my time, there still continued to be time for all church services, as we had done when father was still with us. I had the privilege of teaching a junior Sunday school class, and I believe that I gained more knowledge of the Bible during my preparation for the lessons than I would have in only attending a class.

Studying began to give me a greater compassion for all lost souls. The people of America hear the message over and over again, but ... *how many in other countries have never heard?*

I continued to teach my class with the conviction that God was calling me to foreign missionary work—its persistence I could not understand. Although I enjoyed my class, I was not a public speaker, could not sing or even carry a tune. I felt ...w*hy would the Lord want me?*

The Olive Bethel Church of God about four miles from our home had a revival meeting. Although the message was not about missions, the Holy Spirit spoke to me and gave me such compassion for the lost with a definite Call to be a missionary that I surrendered my life to God in that meeting. I was now, at age 21, willing to do His whole will.

I knew college didn't resume until fall: I'd be 22 by then. I didn't have much money, and knew my mother couldn't help me financially. But I knew that God had called me; that I needed to know more about the Bible; and He would provide a way for me to study.

The dear Godly people at Akron prayed that I would go to Anderson College, their church school. My relatives prayed that I would attend their brand new school, Bethel College (Mishawaka, Indiana), which began its start-up first semester that fall—1947. But one of the men on the Bethel College Board said they never planned on having inner-collegiate athletic sports at Bethel, and my interest in Bethel College ceased: Anderson College became my choice.

I knew very few of my high school courses had been preparatory for college. Finances were a problem. Mother couldn't afford to give me much for the farm work: after I had reached the age of 21, I received $25 a month. It was hard to save anything on this salary. But during the summer we had a good season of baling hay, and I had cleared more than $1,000.00.

In the fall of 1947 I enrolled at Anderson College; Robert started at Purdue University; and Eldon enrolled at Manchester College. Robert and Eldon both took advantage of schooling under the G.I. Bill of Rights because of their military service: we rented out the farm.

College was hard for me. I didn't go out for sports, but enjoyed watching the home games. I had my money budgeted for tuition and other expenses—food, the biggest expense. I planned on one good meal a day, and had lunch here and there for the other meals with no extra money for dates. Besides that, I was extremely bashful around girls, and not interested in marriage. At times, I even thought perhaps I should go to the mission field as a single man. Our daily chapel was held about two blocks from the College. I don't remember walking any girl to or from chapel. In fact, you might have called me "a loner", although I participated in several different group activities.

Every Sunday morning I went with a group that held jail services; played inner-mural basketball with another group; and got together with a third group for a daily vesper, or prayer, service. The remainder of the time I spent in the classroom or studying in the library. Every chance I had on weekends and holidays I went home to help on the farm—about 100 miles away. I don't remember going to any social event or party that first year at Anderson College.

The renters didn't work out on the farm. So I agreed with my mother to come back home to manage the farm; transfer to Manchester College; and commute the 18 miles to college. In this way she furnished me with the family car and gas, along with board and room.

Now I had to discipline my activities more than ever. It was impossible for me to attend, or keep up with, the many athletic events at College or in the local high school of my siblings. But I remained very active in the local church at Akron. With the help of my younger brothers and sisters, we managed the farm during this second year of college.

In the fall of 1949 my older brother, Robert, went into partnership with mother on the farm. Our local church people prayed, urging me to return to Anderson College. This didn't seem possible until late in the baling season: we baled a couple big fields of hay and straw. Upon receiving this money I had nearly as much money as I had when I started my freshman year. At the last minute I enrolled again at Anderson College.

Studying all the time became quite tiresome, so I decided to go out for football. I had only seen a few games in my life. But the coach took one look at me and prepared me to play defense in the center of the line. In my uniform I tipped the scales at 225 lbs—a strong looking player, carrying no extra fat.

On offense, I practiced for the tackle position. At first they pushed me all over the field: the line coach could never get me angry at the other players. I wanted to stop the play, but not hurt the ball carrier. One time—in practice—there were two offense players between me and the halfback as he took a handoff through the line. I reached out and grabbed him just above the ankle. He really went down. The coach said it "looked like Ummel was catching chickens."

Since our left tackle was also our extra point kicker, I took his place every time we scored a touch down. As the year progressed, I often went in on the defense team.

During the football season I had a big appetite and couldn't skimp on my meals. By the end of the season more than half of my summer savings had disappeared. I knew that I had to get a job or I couldn't finish the school year.

Then came the second grading period, and it was hard for me to believe my grades. I had tried so hard and was sure I had done alright. But since my grade "was right on the line", they gave me the lower grade "to make me try harder."

Well, that was not the effect it had on me. I became discouraged, and also disillusioned that Christian teachers could be so heartless. I felt that no one seemed to care about the hardships I had to go through to get to college in the first place, and the genuine effort I had made after being out of school for several years.

Again I went to God—He was "my refuge and my strength." I felt that I certainly had enough reason to lose faith in man, and decided more than ever that it was best to be "a loner."

Manchester College was on the trimester system, and ready to start a new term. After picking up my Anderson College sweater, I packed all my books and clothes, and went home. The next morning I walked into the office of the Dean and President at Manchester College.

They told me I couldn't be registered at two colleges, and needed a *Withdrawal Approval* from Anderson College. A couple hours later I walked into the Dean's office at Anderson.

I confess, I wasn't in any spirit to rethink my decision. The Dean said that he could arrange a loan for me to finish my school year. I replied that I could not borrow money to go to school because I wasn't getting my schooling in order to earn more money later. I would probably earn much less after finishing college since I knew I had been called by God for missionary work. If God wanted me to continue my studies, money would be provided.

Then he told me that someone had sent him a letter stating if I ever needed any financial help, this person had promised to help me.

Well, it was a little late to tell me this. Again my faith in man went to an all-time low. Someone thought they had made provision, only I learned of it too late. I returned to Manchester College yet that afternoon, and registered.

Robert gladly accepted my assistance on the farm. He was happy to have me around just to keep the machinery in running order. In fact, one of the tractors wouldn't start at that particular time. I still had sufficient funds to pay my tuition, and Robert agreed to furnish the gas for me to commute to North Manchester. I only missed one day of school in this transfer between colleges, and helped on the farm as much as possible.

The remainder of my college education worked out very well. I knew that my brother was taking care of the farm. However, I worked many hours. With the new model C Allis Chalmers tractor which had lights, I finished planting our spring oats at midnight.

It wasn't easy to work late in the fields, prepare my lessons for the next day, and keep alert in class. But very seldom did I go to a class without having my lesson well prepared. In that way I was prepared for the final test without an all-night cramming session as many other students did.

The summer of 1950 Eldon sold his share of the baler to me. More automatic balers were coming into our area: we had competition. I had a very good summer, and was able to buy a 1949 Plymouth with about 15,000 miles on it and still have enough money to pay my tuition at college. I continued that fall at Manchester—finishing my Junior year. But because of playing football the previous year at Anderson College—another Conference School—I was ineligible to play at Manchester. However, the coach permitted me to suit up for practice. I played against my brother, Eldon, who was on the starting team. With football practice in the evenings and early morning classes, I studied afternoons taking advantage of the college library.

By this time Eldon had married. He and his wife (Fluella) had an apartment on campus, and always invited me to come over anytime I cared to come. Fluella taught school during the day, so I felt free to go there knowing I would not be disturbing anyone.

As my major was Bible and Philosophy, Eldon and I were never in the same classes, or used the same books. I used the library for studying, and got to know it better than any other place on campus. That year two neighbor boys enrolled at Manchester. After the football season ended, the three of us rode together each day.

By 1951 several more new balers made more competition during the hay season. However, I still had enough satisfied customers and friends that I could keep busy. I returned to Manchester in the fall for my last semester, and became a starter on the football team—left tackle on the offense, and the center of the line on defense. I finished

my college requirements in November, and waited for the graduation ceremonies in May 1952.

The Bible classes had not been easy. I had to study to take my spiritual stand. A small group of us met regularly for a Bible class, and
we had very close fellowship on campus. Although I had more of
an evangelical background, I have always had a real appreciation
for Manchester College, and encountered more people manifesting
the fruit of the Spirit in that place than in most churches. The Lord
was showing me that the church, or pastor, has more responsibility
to give spiritual nurture to families than to over emphasize just the
winning (conversion) of individuals in the depths of sin.

Many pastors preach messages to the people who are *not* sitting
in the pew. Too many messages have been based on evangelism with
little spiritual food for the Christians who need training and guidance. If the Christians would live like they should and manifest love,
there would be a much better normal growth of the church. *Why
should the evangelical churches not have more interest in the social
conditions in the world? ...and the liberal churches have their thrust
almost entirely on the social welfare of the world?*

God had called me to be a missionary in the heart of South America,
and I felt a real interest in Brazil. At every opportunity I went to
hear a missionary from there, or else read books regarding that area.
Everything seemed to confirm this Call. To work in that area more
schooling would be to my advantage—not necessarily seminary—
but rather to get training from a more evangelistic viewpoint.

Bethel College in Mishawaka, Indiana had some excellent Bible
teachers, and I had grown up in that denomination until 15 years of
age. Three of my cousins attended Bethel—one was the secretary
of the Registrar of the College. She invited me to come as a special
student, and pick out only the Bible subjects that I wanted.

This appealed to me. Also, one of the fellows with whom I
had commuted to Manchester College—Cyril Brooke—attended
Bethel. Cyril had become dissatisfied with the spiritual impact at
Manchester, and I had suggested Bethel College to him. Already

living in the dorm, he asked me to be his roommate if I decided to attend Bethel for further Biblical studies.

I arrived at Bethel College in January 1952, and soon discovered God's leading in many ways. At some previous time, a missionary counselor had spoken to all missionary candidates advising us that we should never consider dating—let alone marrying—a girl that didn't also have a missionary Call. Consequently, I had never taken any interest in girls: no girl fit this requirement.

During the first day at Bethel College I met the school nurse— a foreigner from Canada. She stood next to me in line waiting to sign up for classes, and we conversed casually. This in itself was a miracle for me to feel at ease in talking with a young lady.

Upon returning to my room, I asked Cyril about her: "Hey, Dick, she is just the girl for you! She is also heading for the mission field, and is not dating anyone."

Now I thought—*how can I get to know her?* There could not have been a more bashful boy in a college.

The very next day I found the nurse sitting by herself in the library. Nervously I sat down at the same table. To begin the conversation, I told her that I—also—had a Call for missionary work. We talked awhile. But because we were not supposed to talk in the library and I wanted to continue the conversation, I asked her if she would go with me to the basketball game the next Friday night.

The college had several men's and women's teams, and both of us would be playing: an informal date, as we had a carload of students with us. But at least it was a beginning for a bashful, but very assured and determined young man.

Uncle John, my father's brother who had a big dairy farm south of Elkhart, had asked me to help him on the farm in the afternoons and weekends. My three cousins had all called their parents and told them that I had dated the college nurse, Jacquelyn E. McReynolds, from Owen Sound, Ontario, Canada.

On Saturday morning my two uncles, John and James, met me and both wanted to know, "How is the school nurse?" Later I learned that each one of my cousins had a girlfriend that they wanted to introduce to me. But they heartily approved of Jackie and were amazed at how quickly I "fell".

Bethel had strict rules. At that time the girls lived in small homes or cottages—eight girls to each unit. The big yard light at the first cottage set the limit on how far the boys could walk their girlfriends after study hours. After the first date, I walked Jackie to this spot—called "The X"—every night.

The very first Sunday morning at Bethel College a student awakened me early, asking if I would drive him and a group of students to church in Elkhart. His car wouldn't start, and he had promised to take this group with him. The students got into the car—and with them, Jackie. All the others quickly jumped into the car, and the only space left for Jackie was next to me. She was on her way to the Elkhart General Hospital to be a special nurse to the mother of a dorm friend.

After the church service, we passed by the hospital to pick her up, and because our group arrived late for dinner at the College, we were seated at the same table. From then on many other coincidences occurred.

Our interests were the same. We both actively participated in the street meetings held each week in Mishawaka and Niles (a city to the north, just across the Michigan state line). When we went to these meetings, we always had a full carload of students. I made sure Jackie rode in my car and sat beside me. She attended two of my classes, and I could hardly take my eyes off of her. It seemed like a miracle had happened ... *Is it true? ...could it be possible that this lovely young lady also had a genuine missionary Call?*

Within a week of our first date, I told Jackie that God had already shown me that some day we would marry. But as yet, the Lord had not revealed this to her.

This statement surprised her, but she did agree to continue dating me. We could only go out together on double dates. Being a bit older and more mature than most of the other students, we found it quite difficult not to have privacy for serious talks.

When finally one evening she allowed me to kiss her good-night, I knew God was beginning to talk to her, and she was beginning to care for me. Now I wanted my family and friends at Akron to meet Jackie.

It was arranged through the College that if one of my cousins went along, I could take her to my home for a weekend. On our arrival my mother, brothers, and sisters knew something serious was going on: 26 year old Richard had brought a girl home to meet them. Rather shocking, but everyone recovered.

That Saturday evening we had our first date alone, and Jackie accepted my proposal of marriage. Perhaps it was best that we hadn't been able to date alone before. We had known each other only three and one-half months.

On Sunday Jackie went with us to the Akron Church of God. Most of these people knew me personally, and I didn't need to tell them how serious we had become. They immediately accepted her as another in the family of God—just as though I had announced our engagement. Undoubtedly I had a happy expression on my face as I introduced her to our pastor and others.

A week or so later, Jackie's parents visited Bethel on their way from Chicago to Ontario. Jackie's brother, Floyd and his wife Hazel, were driving her parents home. They stopped for a visit and took Jackie out for lunch. In the evening she invited them to meet me. She knew I would be in the library studying at that hour, and had to get permission to call me from my studies. We were under strict rules because both of us had been in responsible positions on campus prior to our engagement. I was glad for the opportunity to meet her parents and part of her family. They, also, sensed the seriousness of our relationship. We felt their approval.

At the end of May we officially announced our engagement with plans to be married August 22 (1952) in the Calvary Missionary Church in Owen Sound, Ontario, Canada. The announcement appeared in the last issue of the Bethel College newspaper. As an engagement gift I gave Jackie a set of silverware. This seemed more appropriate for future missionaries than a diamond, and in keeping with our plans.

Soon after our engagement we purchased a small mobile home—campus married couple style—with arrangements to start making monthly payments in September when we returned to College.

At the close of the school year—early June—I drove Jackie back home to Canada. We started at the break of day to complete the trip in daylight. We wanted to be together as much as possible, but in such a manner that nobody could question our conduct. Besides, I had never been to Canada before, and wanted to see the scenery in the daylight.

Although I could not have been accepted any better by Jackie's parents, it was impossible for me to stay longer than a few days. I needed to bale hay at the farm, and Jackie had a job in the local hospital. When I left the home of her parents, I knew I would not see Jackie again until our wedding in August. It was hard to say good-bye, but we wrote daily and prayed for time to pass quickly.

The summer of 1952 had even less hay for me to bale. I accepted a Scholarship to attend Winona Lake School of Theology. The classes were in the morning, so I could return to the farm when the hay was fully dry, and bale all afternoon. A time came in each day to write a letter to Ontario. Finally the two and one-half months ended, the baling and studies completed, and it was time to return to Canada.

I went one week before our wedding attempting to help Jackie with last minute details of preparation. As she and her family helped me celebrate my 27th birthday, I thanked God for the prospect of soon becoming a part of this loving family who were accepting me so wholeheartedly.

Mother, Eldon and Fluella, Stanley, and Lois, traveled to Ontario for the wedding. Eldon who had been my shadow and a companion in so much of my life, stood beside me as best man. It only seemed appropriate that he become the witness to our marriage.

Mr. & Mrs. Richard L. Ummel
August 22, 1952

Chapter 4

Our Story Together

W e had a short honeymoon before going to Toronto for a visa so Jackie could live in the U.S.A. We finished packing her trunk, loaded all of our wedding gifts and Jackie's belongings in the car, and returned to Indiana with many "things" and very little cash.

Our little mobile home welcomed us back to Mishawaka and we settled in, joining the other married couples at Bethel College. I found a job where I could work the 2nd shift, and return to more Bible studies when the semester began.

By the end of the school year—on June 28, 1953—our first child, Richard Lee, Jr., arrived. He certainly changed our lives, but I felt so proud of that son of ours—now we were three.

Early in 1954—at the invitation of Uncle John and Aunt Ferne—we moved our mobile home about four miles south of Elkhart into the south yard of their farmhouse. Only a short time later—Good Friday afternoon—Uncle John had a bad farm accident with the tractor while pulling stumps in the orchard. Jackie became his special nurse from the first X-rays to the traction harness. Understanding the seriousness of his condition and the need of someone present as he lay on the Stryker frame, Jackie offered to become his night nurse. I had the privilege of assisting my cousin Elaine with the dairy chores and the farming from plowing and planting through to fall harvesting. Their family had always been such a help and blessing to us, so we were thankful to be there to help them in this time of need. Again, God had us in the right place ...*According to HIS Purpose.*

My contacts with Bethel College and the Missionary Church confirmed to me that God wanted me to affiliate with their denomination. We visited the Secretary of the Mission, Rev. Richard Reilly, and explained that although we had fellowship with other churches, we felt that God wanted us to serve with their mission organization, the United Missionary Society (UMS), and that the Lord had been guiding me during a period of time to prepare for mission work in South America—Brazil, especially.

He informed us that if we wanted to go as foreign missionaries we had better have a call to Nigeria, West Africa, which was the main mission field: they had a need for personnel on that Field of service at the time. Reilly also informed us that we would need at least one year of pastoral experience before acceptance.

When the time came for the Annual Indiana Conference, we made ourselves available for a pastorate. Pastoral changes had been made for the year, and we had not been contacted by, or assigned to, any church. I felt led to continue my studies (1953-1955) with the Seminary at Goshen College.

It was a privilege to sit under such dedicated spiritual teachers. At the same time I better understood my cultural background: our family and church had their heritage in that group. But very few of our pastors or missionaries had gone to the Mennonite Seminary. Some people even accused me of "preferring more studies than assuming pastoral duties" to obtain the practical experience the Mission Board recommended. As usual, criticism comes from those who do not know all the facts.

The next year (1954) I again made myself available for a pastorate, but again nothing opened up. I felt God's leading toward more of a Bible teaching ministry. Knowing more study of the Bible wouldn't be amiss, I enrolled for another year at the Seminary.

It wasn't an easy load during the first three years of our marriage, with morning classes followed by a full afternoon of work. First, I delivered coal for the Elkhart County Farm Bureau in Goshen. Most of the memorization of scripture for the classes I did while making rural deliveries of coal. When afternoon classes became necessary,

I found work—second shift—at a factory in Elkhart. Financially, we managed well, but with the required study hours we had little time for social life with other students. School consisted of only classes and the library between classes. Jackie typed many of my term papers, kept busy by keeping house, and caring for our little Ricky. Our second son entered our home on March 6, 1955. We named him Thomas Edward after his two grandpas, and called him Teddy—today he is "Ted".

Early in 1955 the UMS had an interest in starting a work in Brazil, and opened the work in the fall. Several business men had come along beside our denominational leaders and purchased a coffee farm. Because God had called me more than eight years earlier to Brazil, and it appeared extremely difficult to be accepted by the mission to work in Brazil, I thought I should apply as a manager for the farm. I talked this over with Mr. Bontrager, founder of the Christian Stewardship Foundation which had been organized to purchase the coffee plantation.

A call came the next day from Brother Joseph Kimbel who had charge of the Home Mission churches in the Indiana Conference. He told us of a small independent country church close to Argos, Indiana, that needed a pastor. He urged us to go there and speak— presenting ourselves as a pastor—and accept the position if they offered it to me.

I spoke at the church two Sundays: they called me to be their pastor. We moved to the Walnut Gospel Church parsonage in the summer of 1955.

It sounded like a wonderful move and answered our prayer for a church in which to gain experience in order to get to the mission field. We learned many lessons there. Jackie helped in caring for one of our aged members. Through this more than anything else, I feel we got closer to understanding the brethren in the church. I believe this all helped us much more than we, in turn, contributed to the dear people of that community. But continue reading. You will see why the Walnut Church was a bit different.

Because the Walnut Gospel Church was a small church, I helped maintain the church grounds and did the janitorial work. The church had very little, if any, insulation making it difficult to control the heat with the big coal/wood furnace. The church couldn't support us, and work was not available in the area. I continued my job in Elkhart: a drive of about 50 miles one way. Also, we had to fix up the basement parsonage.

The church had started to build a home. When they had the rough floor (sub-flooring) over the basement and covered with tarpaper, a division came into the church and the work stopped. We were grateful they had placed good drains in the floor because after the first rain, water ran in through every wall then escaped through those drains. Cardboard from old cartons that once contained refrigerators and mattresses covered the ceiling. We appreciated having a ceiling, but the first night we found it was full of mice.

Within a few days, Bro. Kimbel had a gathering of Home Mission pastors. These meetings always brought great inspiration to all of us young pastors in spite of any circumstances.

Later, Bro. Kimbel's wife asked Jackie how she liked her new home. Jackie replied, "It is fine, but it would be nice if we had better walls, better ceiling, and a floor."

After laying the (cement block) walls for the basement, they had only pushed the dirt up against the blocks. The dirt settled and the water no longer ran away from the house, but ran toward it. We built up the dirt around the exterior of the foundation, and painted a sealer on the inside of the block walls. No more water came through.

For a kitchen, we installed a kitchen sink and nice cupboards. A pressure water pump was on the premises, and we soon had the bathroom connected up and working. Someone donated an old fuel oil water heater. We hooked it up and had hot running water in the kitchen and bathroom. The automatic part of the heater wouldn't work any more. I lit it daily, and after a couple hours Jackie turned it off: we had hot water all day. The big old space heater would burn either wood or coal and kept the place well heated when we didn't forget to keep it fired up.

We found a big rug for the living room floor. When it rained, we rolled it up so it wouldn't cover the drain. Later we laid some tiles over the kitchen floor, study floor, and part of the living room floor. Of course Ricky, our 2 year old toddler, followed me around—watching and helping—while Teddy would sit propped up watching all that went on.

One day I had a big area of the cement floor covered with black glue for the floor tile. Jackie was helping me while Teddy watched from his baby buggy. Little Ricky came running from his play to show us something. Before we realized what was happening, Ricky ran across that sticky black glue. His feet flew out from under him and he fell, rolling over in the mess. It all happened so fast, and we couldn't do anything but laugh. Even baby Teddy enjoyed the fun. But everything stopped until we got Ricky cleaned up. That sticky glue never came out of his clothes.

We did have a telephone and electricity. Rat poison soon took care of all the mice in the ceiling. A brushing of tar patched the roof. I missed several days of work in order to fix up the house. But soon we had everything in order and fixed up very "homey".

Jackie stayed at home with our two little sons many hours of the day as I drove so far to work. Since childhood she had the desire to play a musical instrument. Eventually we saved enough money to purchase an accordion. After taking only a few lessons, she amazed her music teacher with her progress in playing the instrument.

Then the newly opened field of Brazil needed missionaries, especially those who were ready for pioneer work. I guess we had proved we could make a go of things, even in adverse circumstances. In May of 1956 we formally applied to the UMS and stated our Call at the Annual Meeting held in Brown City, Michigan. The Lord helped so much. I felt His presence so near as He opened my mouth and freed my tongue, banishing my shyness. I was able to impart the deep conviction and desire of my heart. Jackie also stated her Call. After a private interview with the Board, we were accepted: we would leave the U.S.A. in August 1956.

So about a year after our move to Argos, we packed again—but for a much longer move. We sold the furniture and our car, said good-byes to our new friends at the Walnut Gospel Church, and had a lovely farewell service. Members, neighbors, and friends filled the church. How we praised God for their support.

Uncle Paul (Ummel), missionary to Nigeria, came home on furlough that year, and helped us pack. Mainly, he showed us how to pack dishes. We even used the sawdust that he had taken to Nigeria, West Africa, and back again. He seemed happy to see his nephew realizing his Calling. The barrels with our belongings went on ahead to New Orleans. A dear friend loaned us his almost-new Ford station wagon to carry our family and personal baggage to the dock from which the ship would sail. My sister, Joan, accompanied us and drove the vehicle back to Indiana.

**Standing: Robert, Richard, Eldon, Stanley, Herbert, Max
Seated: Phyllis, Lois, Mother, Joan, Carol**

Good-byes are sad in some ways, but we were happy at last to be on our way to the land of our calling. Our two little boys (ages 3 and 1) seemed to sense the excitement and enjoyed it all with us. We stopped at two ports in Brazil—Sao Salvador, and Rio de Janeiro. We felt handicapped without knowing the language, but never-the-less we enjoyed all the highlights and scenery of "Rio". Our desire to learn Portuguese quickly grew stronger every day.

Chapter 5

Into The Brazilian Frontier—1956

After 23 days on the freighter *Del Alba*, we finally arrived at our destination, the Port of Santos, on September 7, 1956—Independence Day in Brazil. Because of the holiday, everything was shut down at the port. Our fellow missionaries, Earl and Dorothy (Dottie) Hartman, rented a little rowboat and came out to meet us. We went ashore with them to see Santos and to visit. Later that afternoon another fellow missionary, Don Granitz, arrived from Campinas to welcome us. We could not communicate with the Brazilians, so Don and Earl helped us through customs.

News of the Frontier and the fast development of the new coffee farm were of utmost interest to us. It was decided that we should go directly to Xambre, a Frontier city in the northwest part of the state of Parana, bordering Paraguay. Teachers would be arranged for us to study the language, and we would become available to help with the Mission work immediately.

Usually it takes several hours to get through customs. For us, it took several days as our baggage was in the bottom of the hold of the ship. The Brazilian custom officials seemed very much surprised that we were going straight to the Frontier, and told us we would need everything we brought with us. As a result, we had very little duty to pay on our baggage. The baggage went by an express company to Maringa, Parana. As soon as the express truck picked up our baggage, we headed for Sao Paulo.

At that time some big old cars from the U.S.A.—special taxi-types with two or three seats—ran regular routes between Santos and Sao Paulo. As soon as they were filled with passengers they took off, and would stop anywhere along the way to drop someone off, and pick up other passengers. Because they left every few minutes, we didn't need to wait very long. Many old buses were available also, but they traveled much slower and sometimes had a long wait for their scheduled run.

This two-hour scenic drive took us up through the mountains into Sao Paulo. What a surprise to see this modern superhighway as we went through these long tunnels. An ancient narrow gauge train track accompanied the road most of the way. "This track," they said, "had been laid during our civil war days, and has had very few changes since then." Wood-burning steam engines powered these trains.

At the end of this 80-100 mile drive, we arrived in the great metropolis of Sao Paulo. I couldn't believe my eyes as I walked through the center of the city. The streets were narrow and made of cobblestone for the horse-and-buggy days of the past—no cars were permitted. Many banks and commercial stores stood in this center. The streets were filled with people almost running in every direction. I almost ran to keep up with Earl as he dodged in and out going down the narrow streets.

We stopped at the large Byington Building. Up on about the 12th floor, I was introduced to the head officials, owners, and developmental engineers for the land colonization out in the state of Parana—the area being opened up for coffee farms. The Group gave us key lots for our church and Mission home in the center of Xambre, Parana.

The States of Parana and Sao Paulo, Brazil

This large company had been an old mining and construction company in Brazil, and they built a railroad for the state of Parana. Since Parana didn't have enough money to settle the account, a large parcel of land (shaded area on the map) had been given to the Byington Company to develop. They were pleased to meet me and to see the interest our Mission had in their area. Later, from time-to-time this top man stopped to visit us in our home at Xambre. We have always kept a very good relationship with these top officials. Our mail for many years came in care of their land office in Maringa. As they brought potential land buyers to the area, they brought our mail to Xambre.

Our church leaders and business men came into contact with this company on their initial trip to Brazil. The Byington Land Company had promised to help our Mission get started in Brazil. They said, if we would build a big church in the center of Xambre, they would donate the ground for the church. In response, the U.S.A. business men of our church came together as the Christian Stewardship Foundation (CSF) and bought about a section of land to develop a coffee farm. The Foundation also promised that all the profits from the farm would be donated toward our missionary work in Brazil.

After meeting these gentlemen, we went to a large bank and exchanged dollars for cruzeiros. This way of handling money has always been a shock to me, but others did the same thing. We had to have a briefcase to carry all our money: no banks out on the Frontier.

Finished here, we caught a taxi and soon were at the airport. Even at this time the city had surrounded the airport. Soon we boarded a Brazilian DC3 plane headed for Londrina, Parana—my first flight. I really enjoyed flying over the rolling country. The pilots flew VFR—visual flight rules. We were not too far above the ground and easily could see that most of this area which had been coffee plantations until the 1930s, now was pasture.

We saw an occasional ranch homestead, and took note of the layout of the tile covered buildings. In the center stood a large Latin-styled home with outlaying buildings which had been slave quarters at one time. The big brick and cement coffee drying areas were still there. Not far from the buildings stood large corrals that handled, and cared for, their large Brahma herds of cattle. Much of the countryside looked almost like wasteland—a permanent pasture where they just let everything grow. But what I had called "wasteland" turned out to be much better pasture than I had thought it to be. I had compared it with our cultivated alfalfa hay fields and improved pasture land in Indiana.

From the plane the dirt roads were easily visible. Every truck or vehicle had a big cloud of dust rolling behind it. I should say—just ahead of each cloud of dust was a vehicle. At times we could see a long cloud of dust with several vehicles in its cloud—so thick we couldn't make out if the vehicles were trucks, Jeeps, or cars.

The state of Parana was a contrast to the state of Sao Paulo. The new coffee fields were neat and beautiful with everything laid out very neatly in parallel rows—only a few on contour. The layout of fields, farms, and roads was much different than I expected. All the main roads were built to follow and stay on top of the ridges of the beautiful rolling land. A stream of water usually became the boundary on the lower side of the farm. Very seldom did they build their homes along the side of the road, but on the lower side near the stream or small rivers with either uncut jungle or pasture on the extreme lowlands. Seldom did I see a rectangular or square field. Many appeared as triangles, or whatever shape fit the rolling country side.

Since no road ran straight but followed the high points of the terrain, it was almost impossible for the front of the farm to have a straight side. Of course, no stream runs straight either. The rolling countryside would be three to ten miles from one hilltop to another, making the farms long and narrow. Most homes stood at least a mile or more from the main road. Adjacent to the small towns and cities the farms became smaller, and the homes much closer to the roads.

I had my camera and took many pictures. It's good that a new missionary does this, for soon everything appears normal as they become used to their new environment.

Within an hour our plane began to circle a modern city—Londrina, meaning "Little London". A British company had developed this area. The same company later became one of the largest land colonization companies in Parana.

In a short time we turned into the drive of the Bible School campus of the OMS (Oriental Mission Society)—called the "Latin American Mission" in Brazil: a beautiful layout. Here the Hartman children had been awaiting the arrival of their parents. That night we had a good visit with everyone, but we were anxious to get to our destination.

The next day we arrived in Maringa. It had rained all night, and mud was everywhere. About an inch of the red clay stuck to our shoes with each step we took, and our shoes became heavier and heavier as we walked.

Teddy couldn't walk in the mess. I carried him. His feet already in the mud, left part of it behind wherever his feet touched my clothes. Every store and home had a big metal block—a scraper—

on the porch to help remove the mud from shoes. Most of the stores scattered sawdust on the floor, making it easier to clean the floor. The sawdust clung to customers' shoes instead of tracking mud on the floor.

The Palace Hotel became our home for the next few days. It rained a little every day and most of each night—no buses or any other vehicles were getting through. About four blocks right in the center of this pioneer town had cobblestone. Almost 20 feet from the beginning of this cobblestone we saw a big truck mired down in the mud—no axle in view—in front of Fuganti, one of the biggest general stores in Maringa. These trucks and cars came from streets and roads which had no gravel on them. They brought this sticky mud onto the good streets, and made one to three inches of sloppy mess on the improved streets. So to us as new missionaries, the Palace Hotel was a paradise. The rooms were plain but tidy, reminding us of the pictures of pioneer days in the U.S.A. Every bed had white sheets and bedspreads. One of the children got on the bed with his shoes still on—what a mess. Needless to say, after that everyone took off their shoes at the door.

With an immediate need to get the work started in Xambre, the Hartmans had studied Portuguese diligently in Campinas, and finished in six months rather than one year. Then they moved to Maringa, closer to the Xambre area, and had radio connections with Xambre through the Byington Land Company office. After about five months in Maringa, and only two weeks before our arrival in Brazil, they moved to Xambre. They didn't have their home completely in order yet when they came to meet us at Santos.

Earl knew Maringa quite well and purposely had us staying in the Palace Hotel located in close proximity to the Byington offices. I accompanied Earl to their offices several times a day to get the news from Xambre to hear if there were any vehicles getting through on the roads.

While delayed here we saw and learned more about the city. Maringa was the central shopping center of the northwestern part of the state. Most of the food supplies, furniture, vehicles, garages, auto parts, and other stores, had their headquarters in Maringa. In 1956 they had very few branch stores west of here.

Maringa was the end of the line for train service. People by the hundreds were camped out in the train station awaiting trucks to take them on to where they would be settling. Many of these people bought supplies before heading further west. We, too, had time to purchase many staple foods and supplies, order furniture, and get parts for the old Jeep. No place west of here had bottle gas—it too came from Maringa. Later we found out that fresh vegetables and fruits, also, were unavailable in the western towns beyond Maringa.

About the third day we began getting "cabin fever". The children— six of them between four months and five years old—were too confined in these small quarters. Also the hotel bill grew daily. Each day had some bright sunshine, but it rained every night.

We learned that the Land Company began sending their prospective land buyers out in a small airplane which held three adults in addition to the pilot. Earl knew the Xambre area had a more sandy soil, making the runway safe for landing. He arranged a truck to pick up our baggage coming from Santos to Maringa, and also the furniture and supplies we had purchased. It would all be transported to Xambre when the roads opened again. He then arranged two small planes to take our two families to Xambre: this held another first experience, flying in a small airplane.

Our eyes opened wide again to take in the new scenery and the new country that would become our home. My camera clicked a lot. Soon after we left Maringa the whole rolling countryside became virgin timber—like a huge green carpet. The road we followed became just a narrow trail through the jungle. Where the timber had been cut, coffee already had been planted. At that time everyone had only the planting of coffee on their mind. Some other crops such as corn, beans, and rice, were planted between the straight rows of coffee.

As we approached the new pioneer villages, more land had been cleared. Every time we saw a stream crossing the road, we would see long lines of trucks which couldn't make it up the steep incline after crossing the narrow wooden bridges. Flying over Cianorte we could see that from there on, the vehicles crawled along more slowly over the roads. After we crossed the large River Ivai, the soil appeared more sandy, or a mixed soil with much less of that sticky clay stuff. Although we saw many deep ruts in the road, they were getting through. As we passed over Umuarama we could see Xambre on the horizon. At that time these two towns were about the same size.

About 30 minutes after leaving Maringa, our two planes were approaching the Xambre airport. First they circled, buzzing the small village so the Jeep-taxi would come out to pick us up. The airport, however, was only a small clearing that at first glance looked like a wide spot in the road about a mile from Xambre. As soon as we crossed the Xambre River we landed on this airport going uphill. We stepped out of the plane feeling like we were at the end of the world—so far from home and our loved ones. It had taken us 38 days from Indiana to Xambre.

It was getting late, and the plane needed to get back to Maringa before dark. A few men rushed out to board the two planes for the return flight. Before we had our hand baggage in the Jeeps, the planes were up in the sky headed back to civilization. This was the end of the run: Xambre. Only the deep assurance that God had called us to this place kept us from despair as we looked at what would be our new home. In reality: as yet—there was no home for us.

We drove up in front of Hartman's home. It had been very difficult while living in Maringa to supervise construction of the Mission home in Xambre. Temporarily Earl had rented a worker's house from the Byington Company in which to live.

This simple wooden house measured only 6 meters by 8 meters (19.6 ft. x 26.2 ft.), counting both the front and back porches. With no other house available to rent, and having to wait at least two weeks for our furniture and baggage, we all lived together in that tiny house. We sensed close fellowship in Christ among us; and knew that God had called all of us to this place. The Hartmans seemed happy to have us with them, and we were certainly happy they were with us in this far away place. We had very little friction considering the small quarters with the children—remarkable. We all got to know each other very well.

Within a short time we began studying language from Sr. Bosco, the Company radio operator. In this way we also were informed of planes and Jeeps coming through, plus hearing some world news. His wife, Zoe, was the school teacher and began teaching Portuguese to Jackie. It took so much time just to exist in these pioneer conditions—prepare meals, wash clothes, and other chores—that we didn't have much time to study.

The stores had only small mounts of canned foods, and hardly any fresh fruits or vegetables. With no pasture in the area, the cattle had to be driven in. Many had been on the road for as long as 30 days. When butchered, their meat wasn't the best. Even with the pressure cooker it was as tough as rubber.

The stores stocked beans and rice, the staple food of most Brazilians. We learned to fix that. It became—even to this day—the favorite of our children. The small game and birds that the men killed in the jungle supplemented their diet. Occasionally we were given some of this game meat. We didn't care for it enough to buy more.

Our water came from a deep—120 ft—well. We pulled it up by hand on a windlass rope and bucket. For drinking water, it had to go through the filter. This filter, made from baked clay, stood about 2 feet in the air, and held about 3 gallons of water. We never accumulated a big supply of water, and many times we had a line-up waiting for water as it dripped through the filter.

An outside toilet received regular use. Later I heard that our neighbors laughed at the steady use our toilet had. Both families getting used to both the water and food caused us much dysentery.

After many hours of washing clothes by hand each week, we decided to send most of it out. As I heard the wash lady rubbing and batting my pants on a wooden washboard, I didn't expect them to return in one piece. This type of washing took much of the life out of our clothes.

With Teddy still in diapers, Jackie washed the diapers and some of our white clothes on our own scrub board. Clothes surely didn't take long to dry in that hot sunshine. Our washer lady and other neighbors hung their clothes on a barbwire clothesline: they didn't need clothespins. But if there was much wind, our clothes had little three-corner tears in them. Some of the washer ladies sewed up these holes if they were too big. We learned to say, *In all things give thanks.*

No doctor lived within 2 hours drive of Xambre. The Land Company had built a house for a doctor, but he had gone back to Rio de Janeiro for a vacation. The head of the Company, Dr. Aldo, soon found out that my wife was a registered nurse from Canada. After only a few days they called Jackie to check on some ladies that were expecting babies: Dottie Hartman went along to interpret.

The midwives of the area had no practical training and most of them would be considered almost as witch doctors. On these occasions Earl usually drove the old Jeep and I stayed with the children. A few times I drove and he stayed home.

One of these early calls took us to the Fazenda (farm) Ouro Verde, home of a Japanese owner who had grown up in Brazil. Through this contact he invited us to hold religious services on his farm, and many of our early converts came from this farm.

The Christian Stewardship Foundation (CSF) had purchased a section of land in the Xambre area—about 30-45 minutes beyond Xambre. Don Granitz had the responsibility of developing and managing this big farm in addition to his missionary duties. The Foundation's Brazilian farm manager drove their big truck into Maringa to get workers.

In those first days men came west to make big money. A lot of men came without their family—planning to return later to bring the family back with them. Many of these men came from the north-eastern states of Brazil where the drought had driven them away from that area. They came by train to Maringa and picked up jobs with landowners who sent their trucks into the city for workers. The men hired by the CSF farm had been brought more than 200 kilometers (approximately 125 miles) west to help work and develop the farm.

After purchasing the farm a pioneer work crew arranged to cut the trees out of the jungle, burn them off, and plant the coffee beans in 10 inch deep holes with protection from the sun. Later, some of these men went back for their family. By the time I first visited the farm, the Brazilian farm manager had about a dozen families and many single men taking care of the farm.

The CSF farm, Fazenda Peroba, became one of our first preaching points. Every time we went there we had 50-100 people in the services. Later it became our strongest Sunday school and church in Brazil. They built a large church on the premises and many neighbors from a radius of several miles attended.

Very few landowners lived on their farms. Most of them lived in the bigger cities or another farm back east. These Frontier people who moved into the area were day workers or share-croppers. Although the big farms had a farm manager, most of the owners of smaller farms preferred to turn the land over to share-croppers because the share-croppers didn't need as much supervision. Various types of contracts were made to the workers.

If the renter took on a six-year contract, he would be expected to cut the virgin timber; plant and develop the land for coffee crops; and make his own simple shelter in which to live. During the six years everything he raised was his own, and he could plant other crops between the rows of coffee. By the end of the sixth year they could expect to have full-sized mature coffee bushes.

Usually the entire family would enter into the project. Even children five or six years of age had their responsibilities. Many of these types of share-croppers would have enough money after the completion of their contract to buy their own small farm. But it was hard for them in the beginning with no crop of coffee until at least the fourth or fifth year. They lived only from the crops planted between the rows: corn, beans, and rice. Usually the sixth year produced their first big crop of coffee.

The bigger farms gave four-year contracts to their share-croppers. In a four-year contract the land would have been cleared out and planted in coffee. The share-croppers cared for the coffee, and could also plant between the rows. These crops belonged to the workers. After caring for the coffee four years, the workers could renew their contracts yearly for 40% or 50% of the crop.

Many of these workers—as on the Fazenda Peroba farm—were loaned money to exist until they could pay back with their harvest. Most of the big and poorer families preferred this type of contract, and many were able to purchase their own small farm after four to six years of labor.

Earl—an extrovert—soon knew all of the key men of the area, and could call all these big landowners by name when they came to town. In a short time he had permission to hold religious services on most of the large farms of the area. He also became acquainted with the politicians and leaders who, usually, were the owners of the new sawmills.

Even though the Mission house and church were not built as yet, we held nightly services all over the area. Many of these farms and sawmills required an hour or more of driving time. Usually we left home about 4:30 p.m. to go to the service. Allowing time to visit before and after each service, we usually didn't get home until nearly midnight. At times we all went. It crowded the Jeep. But often Jackie stayed at home with the children while I went with Earl. I usually gave a short testimony, and Earl translated for me.

Between times Earl arranged for lumber to be cut and delivered for the Mission house. As many people needed lumber, we had to continually urge the owner to "cut the next logs for us." On most of these trips I had the privilege of accompanying Earl.

We enjoyed our life on the Frontier. The fellowship of our two families brought us closer in the spirit of our Lord, and we felt like one big family—a good feeling as we all felt so far from our own relatives.

Byington had many vehicles coming out with land buyers which brought our mail from the U.S A. every 10-14 days. We enjoyed hearing from home. The sharing of mail helped us become acquainted with each other's family.

A couple weeks after our arrival, our baggage and furniture arrived. Another new house had been built in town, and became available for rent the day before our things came. We did some finishing-up touches to the house as we settled in. Again it became difficult to find time to do Bible and language study. But by using a few words, sign language and pointing, we did our own shopping. The clerks had patience and many laughs at our expense, and other shoppers came in to watch us make our purchases. We just laughed with them and developed a great love for them because of their patience and friendliness.

We thought everything worked out perfectly. Now we had our own home. But it became more difficult to find time for the language study, and we could not attend quite as many of the evening services. Occasionally the Hartman children stayed in our house until their parents returned from a service.

Then the unexpected happened.

Chapter 6

Why, Oh Why, Lord?

O n October 28, 1956, I became ill with a high fever and great pain. A doctor had returned to the area. He gave me pain medicine, but it didn't help. He sent us on a three-hour drive to Cruzeiro de Oeste—the nearest hospital.

The Company loaned Earl their pickup truck and put a mattress in the back for me to lie on. Only one glance at the truck and mattress, and I knew I wouldn't be able to stand the ride over those rough roads. So I insisted on sitting in the cab with Earl and Jackie. At midnight we pulled up in front of the hospital.

We clapped our hands a short time, and the doctor came to the door. He carried a little candle and wore a long night shirt, looking like the *Jack Jumped over the Candlestick* picture that I had seen in my first grade class. Even though sick and weak, I almost laughed at his appearance.

Soon they had me on the second floor of the house lying on a mattress filled with cornhusks. The doctor had a Coleman kerosene pressure lantern that lit up the room brightly. Later I could hear the hiss of the lantern as he came up the stair steps and down the hall to our room. He immediately began to give me many shots. When I turned over and stretched out in a different position my foot hurt, and I told Jackie.

Tired and a little exasperated she said, "How could the pain now be in your foot?" and calmly took the candle down to examine my foot: it was bleeding. A broken ampule (glass container for a dose of medicine) was the culprit. It had missed the waste basket at the foot of the bed.

When we married, I gave Jackie a wedding ring, but didn't want one for myself since many in our church at that time did not wear wedding rings. It's customary in most Brazilian hospitals for two beds to be in one room: an extra one for a relative to use during their stay with the patient to help care for them.

Earl had gone to sleep on the extra bed with his baseball cap over his eyes. We let the candle burn all night, and Earl's left hand quite visibly displayed his wedding ring. After having the shots I finally rested, and my wife was curled up on the edge of my small bed. When the nurse came in to check me, she saw Earl's ring and Jackie's ring.

Jackie responded, "Meu marido (my husband)". The nurse just sort of laughed, or sneered, in the face of my wife. Later when I had an opportunity, I bought a ring for myself—and I wear it, too.

After I was supposed to be "settled down" another Jeep pulled up in front of the hospital. They clapped for the doctor.

It turned out to be an emergency appendectomy and the doctor did the surgery in the room directly below mine. With only one-inch thick flooring we heard the entire conversation, and even the burning lantern. The many moans allowed my imagination to run wild. Afterward the doctor came up the stairs to show us his success. He carried the lantern in one hand and held the appendix in the other—blood all over it.

I felt much better by morning and wanted to get out of there. We asked the doctor what he thought caused my illness. He said that he didn't know, but that one of the shots must have helped. Two days later we went back to Xambre.

The following week the pain came back—much worse. The Company radio was not functioning, and they could not contact Maringa to send a plane. More rain prevented even the Jeeps from getting through to send a message out to Maringa. We prayed for God to take over the situation.

For about a half hour the sun came out, and the sky cleared. A small uncharted plane buzzed the town to call a Jeep to come to the airport. Earl, also, went to the airport in the Mission Jeep, and arrived before the town Jeep-taxi.

A potential land buyer had come to Xambre. They said we could fly back with the plane if we could "be ready to leave in 5 or 10 minutes ... the clouds were beginning to close in again." By the time Earl returned, Jackie already had our small suitcase packed. We felt confident that God sent that plane.

Within the hour I was in the Maringa Hospital. But again the pain left. After the doctor examined me, he ordered an X-ray of my urinary tract. The X-ray equipment was not in the hospital. Each doctor had his own hospital with the X-ray equipment in a centrally located private home about a block from this particular hospital. At this central location each of the doctors had access to the shared equipment.

Since I had no pain, I walked with Earl to have the X-ray taken. The doctor hadn't found anything wrong with me, so I went with Earl to buy supplies to take back to Xambre. We used the hospital room like a hotel room.

After almost an hour of walking around town, I felt a little tired and went back to our hospital room to rest. On his way back, Earl picked up the X-ray and gave it to the doctor.

As soon as Earl entered our room, I asked, "How soon are we going back to Xambre?"

Earl seemed worried, as if he didn't know how to approach the subject, then said, "You are just to rest here. A plane is taking me back to get Jackie, and the same plane is taking us to Sao Paulo to the Samaritan Hospital."

I could hardly believe my ears: I had no pain anymore. But Earl went on to say that "the X-ray showed only one kidney" and "it was two to three times the normal size ... the ureter had greatly enlarged with almost a complete blockage as it entered the bladder."

I rested in Maringa until Earl came back from Xambre with Jackie. She had left our boys with Dottie, and came quickly.

The flight to Sao Paulo was beautiful, but we didn't talk much. I guess trying to fathom the meaning of all of this occupied our minds. The closer we came to Sao Paulo, the more we realized we were coming back to civilization.

As soon as they admitted me to the hospital, I went for X-rays again—confirming the Maringa doctor's diagnosis. The doctor gave me a treatment and medication, and said he wanted to see me again in 10 days.

Don Granitz came from Campinas to visit us at the hospital. Upon the doctor's release, we went to Don and Jean's home for the week. We enjoyed getting to know them and their two small children. After another two days at the hospital, we returned to Xambre.

Life in Xambre soon was back to the routine, except our little boys just clung to us and wouldn't let either one of us of their sight. Once again it took so much time just to exist that we didn't find much time to study language—all our water had to be pulled up by hand from the deep open well; we walked to buy our supplies as Earl needed the Jeep to visit and go to the services; cooking food took much longer than in the U.S.A.; we had no washing machine, and couldn't use the electric iron; plus the daily chore of cleaning the kerosene lamps and pressure lantern.

The first time we arrived in Xambre—the brand new pioneer town— every tree in the area designated for the future city had been cut down. First they cut the underbrush and then they dropped the trees on top of this brush using only axes and crosscut saws. In order to begin construction they used the Byington Company's bulldozer to push these logs to one side. They were too green to burn.

A couple months after our arrival, they announced their plan to burn these logs and underbrush off the Xambre area. As the smoke began to get thick, Earl and his family drove up with the Jeep and said, "Let's go to Umuarama and get out of this smoke."

It didn't take us long to get ready. As we drove along the road we could see the smoke billowing up in the sky.

After several hours (and toward evening) we headed back to Xambre. Everything in our house was covered with about one inch of ashes—everything, including the floor. The ashes had been blown, or drifted, into the house as we did not have window glass in the windows. Most logs and stumps were still burning and smoldering.

This continued for a week until the next big rain. Much smoke lingered in the air, our eyes stayed red, and the smoke bothered our breathing for days.

These burnings became a regular and normal inconvenience for several months as they cut the jungle around us. With less jungle, we had many less insects. I am not sure if the smoke killed them off, or they just moved farther back into the jungle. We even had less big spiders.

The day the Xambre Mission house was finished, Hartmans moved in. It stood on a hill at the edge of town. At the same time the church grounds were in the process of being cleared with plans in the process to build a church.

The Granitz family moved from Campinas to Xambre just before Christmas. Here Don would be closer to supervise the Fazenda Peroba (CSF farm) and help in the Mission work. Providentially another larger house in Xambre became available to rent. Since Don and his family planned to move to the farm as soon as possible, they moved in where we and the Hartman family had been staying, and our family moved into the larger house.

Our first Christmas in Brazil became a very busy time. Since the Hartmans hadn't had any vacation during their time in Brazil, and because two of their children were ill, they left for a two-week rest and recuperation time. I knew the location of the scheduled farm services, and Don Granitz could take charge of the services. But plans changed.

A few days after Earl left, Lori — the Granitz's baby girl — became ill and had to be flown to Maringa. This left our family in Xambre to spend our first Christmas in Brazil alone. We had such a feeling of sadness — alone and far away from home — yet we praised God that the four of us were together and well.

We had brought with us from the U.S.A. our Christmas bulbs and decorations, and we decided to have a tree. Upon asking, the sawmill manager told us where we could locate a pine tree outside the town. We drove out on the jungle road to find our tree.

Finally we spotted the tall pines on a distant knoll. With great difficulty I managed to get through the underbrush to the trees. The young trees were extremely spindly because of the dense underbrush, but I cut one out that stood about six feet tall.

Emerging from the jungle with my prize, I discovered it seemed very flexible. Jackie had her doubts about how to fix it up, and by the time we reached home it looked sicker than ever. The limbs did not have the strength to hold our decorations, and each branch sagged to the floor.

It looked so bad the next morning that I took the tree out and threw it on the smoldering logs near our house where the Company men had just burned off more land for expansion of the city of Xambre.

When the boys awakened and found the tree gone, they were so sad. Without electricity, we strung the light bulbs and decorations around the windows of our home just to decorate. But our three-and-one-half-year-old Ricky cried and cried: Daddy had burned the promised Christmas tree. Although it had looked terrible to us, our boys had accepted it as our Christmas tree—droopy and all.

Christmas morning we went to the parsonage of the Hartmans and used their Maytag washing machine with a gas motor—washing on Christmas just to keep busy. Since Don Granitz had given us permission to use their new Chevrolet pickup truck. We decided to pack a lunch and drive out to the Parana River, about 90 kilometers (56.25 miles) west of Xambre.

What a beautiful drive going on this narrow trail through the jungle. Only about one-sixth of the jungle between Xambre and Perola had been cut along the road. Even that hadn't been cut more than one kilometer from the road.

Perola had only three or four buildings. Between Perola and Porto Byington on the Parana River, only three places had been cut out from the jungle. The road was a narrow trail just wide enough for one vehicle without getting off the trail into the jungle. Each small waterhole in the road had clouds of colorful butterflies, in addition to the many big beautiful butterflies that flew constantly in the jungle.

Byington had used heavy equipment to make their roads level with no stumps. A vehicle could drive right along. The Company had first mapped out the area from their airplane photography. Then engineers and a work crew went in to cut the trees. After this, the big bulldozers and heavy road equipment made the trails through the jungle. As more traffic came into the area, they made the trails wider. But the more jungle that they cut, the more erosion problems they had in keeping these roads open.

Today it was Christmas—no other vehicle on the road—and no Byington vehicles brought out land buyers. In one spot on the road we hit some loose sand. The motor stopped. I knew it was unlikely that any other vehicle would pass this way before New Year's Day. We prayed that God would help me to find the trouble.

Soon the small flies and gnats began to attack us in swarms, leaving painful itchy bites on all of us. I knew the motor stopped as though it had drowned out by water, which had happened many times. When I took the distributor cap off, sand fell out. I cleaned it the best I could, and the motor started immediately. How we praised God for helping us find the trouble: He is always faithful.

The beautiful Parana River appeared to be almost a mile across, and its current moved right along. Later we were informed that we did not see the other side of the River. We had seen a big island more than ten miles long, and "the River is wider on the other side of the island." None of the virgin forest had been cut on either side as far as we could see on the horizon. Byington had built a resort house but only a caretaker lived there, and the family had gone to Sao Paulo for the Christmas-New Year vacation period.

We felt it a real privilege to take the trip out to the River and back. Had we stopped in the jungle at any place along the way, we could have said that we were the "first white man" to stop on that spot. The underbrush was so thick it would have been impossible to see a wild animal or a bird ten feet from the trail. They can hear the vehicle coming, and enter the jungle to be hidden.

A person can do a lot of traveling on these Frontier roads and see very little of the wildlife. If we would stop at a waterhole, there would be many small animal tracks. Most of the wildlife in Brazil consists of wild pigs, a species of the raccoon family, small deer, and oncas (jaguars).

The hunters usually crawl up in a tree close to a stream or pond to stalk the game. But the underbrush is so thick and the animals blend in so well that it is almost impossible to spot them until they move or come out in an opening. Some men have hunted with dogs attempting to drive the game up the trails where a hunter awaits.

An onca is very hard to hunt and kill. They are sly and can outrun the dogs. Usually they will stay just ahead of a pack of dogs. As the leading dog gets closer, they wait and kill the leader, continually doing this until there are no more dogs. If a hunter knows their dogs are chasing an onca, they will attempt to call them off. This becomes almost impossible because the dogs soon get out of calling range.

Many of the oncas have been killed as they sneak up to kill and eat small pigs or other farm animals. The Frontiersmen wait for them to come back for more livestock. I heard about one man who killed one of these big spotted cats with a butcher knife. There have been many rumors of a "killer onca" in the area. But in my 22 years on the Frontier, I have never heard of an onca attacking any person. As long as there is game or domestic animals, they will not bother humans. However, when in self defense, they could be very dangerous. A few times a hunter caught a cub after its mother had been shot.

As the jungle is cut, the oncas retreat. Several times I have seen their tracks along the road, but have never seen a wild one alive, except in the circus or in a zoo.

Before going to the Frontier of Brazil, I had planned to always carry a revolver or rifle with me. But when I got there I realized that I would be safer without any arms as many criminals lived among these first settlers. After escaping the law, the Frontier became their safest place. These criminals were so much faster and a better shot that there would not have been any chance of defending myself. I considered my Bible my protection and sword.

Nearly all the Frontiersman carried either a knife or gun for protection against snakes and animals in the jungle. They usually accompanied us as we traveled through the jungle trails. However, our greatest confidence, by faith, came from God's protection.

The big wild animals in Brazil did not worry us. The small insects and parasites became an inconvenience. Along the streams and in the jungle, the small blood-biting flies and gnats would attack in swarms. When the marching ants came through we had to just get out of their path. As these ants began to come through our house, we made sure all our food supplies were sealed in containers, and then just got out. The ants would actually kill and eat all the cockroaches, spiders, and other bugs in the house.

In fact, when we noticed the spiders and cockroaches crawling out of their hiding places, we recognized it as a good sign that the ants were on their march. If it happened at night with the children in bed, we quickly splashed kerosene around their bed, and the house. They never crossed over the kerosene, but went around it. I don't know how they passed the word along their ranks, but they communicated and it worked. Should they find any food, they all congregate around it, and will evade kerosene or other poisons.

One time in the middle of the night, our little daughter Anita awakened screaming. Her bed sat next to the wooden wall. Ants completely covered her, even her hair, and they were biting her. Immediately we undressed her and put her in the bathtub.

The jungle has many big tarantula spiders. In the more civilized part of Brazil they live mostly in the banana groves—many people call them *the banana spider.*

But at Xambre the jungle was very close to our home. Inside our house we killed one or so tarantula spiders every week. With no electricity, we always slept with a flashlight under the edge of our pillow. Many times Jackie would awaken me declaring she heard a spider go up the wall.

At first I just laughed at her saying, "Jackie, it's impossible to hear a spider walk!" However, she was always right. We would flash the light and there it would be, and I would get up and kill him with the broom.

One time we came home late at night. As I lit the pressure lantern Ricky yelled, "Look, a big spider is dead on the floor." Quickly I warned everyone that he was "only sleeping", and killed him. With its legs spread out, it covered a space the size of Jackie's hand. But sleeping, they look like a fuzzy ball.

If they were on the ceiling, I always used a chair to stand on, and hit them with the broom in order not to be directly below them. Several times they jumped at me just before the broom hit them, and I've felt their hairy bodies brush my face before quickly knocking them to the floor with my hand. We have to be alert as they can jump about a meter (39+ inches). The Brazilians have a great fear of the tarantula.

I know of one young girl that accidently stepped on one. Immediately someone gave her a shot to counteract the poison. Even with the shot she became very ill with a high fever for nearly a week, and had an ugly sore at the site of the bite. Actually the spider does try to get away from humans by jumping, and the poison is for the purpose of killing prey for its meal as well as protection. The tarantula's flexible body can get through a smaller hole or crack in the wall than a tiny mouse.

The *bicho de pe* is another small insect belonging to the flea family. They wiggle into feet and under toenails and fingernails to lay eggs. A little capsule forms, and will grow and grow if not removed. If they are not removed soon after entering, they become quite large, and after removal a hole is left sometimes a quarter of an inch in diameter.

After only a few weeks in Xambre we discovered these spots on our boys' feet. We removed several each day. They never went barefooted again, but still we continued to be plagued by these small painful insects. The boys began dreading bath time—it meant *bicho removal time*. But as the country became more populated causing the cutting down of more jungle, we had less problems with its insects.

We had a constant battle with fleas. Jackie regularly put flea powder in our beds to prevent their visits. An empty or abandoned house is a perfect setting for the multiplication of fleas. The dry sand and dirt under the houses help them thrive well. Most of the fleas were picked up when coming in contact with other people on the buses, in their homes, and in the services. If someone had a cat, dog, or other animal in or around the house, most of the fleas will go to them rather than to humans. Our pets needed regular baths and treatments. The Brazilians have very beautiful hardwood and ceramic floors which are waxed regularly. Most households use a wax with flea repellant or poison in it. So you see, it's a constant battle.

Needless to say, we had a very busy life getting accustomed to the Frontier environment which limited our time with language. But we already had made many friends, enjoyed conversations with them and living in our new larger house.

In two months I returned to the hospital in Sao Paulo for my scheduled checkup, although I felt very well and had experienced no pain. Don and I made the trip, leaving our wives and children in Xambre. The X-rays showed the stricture in my ureter had not improved. The doctor was ready to operate and replace my only ureter with a plastic one. We couldn't accept that as yet, and flew back to share the news regarding the proposed operation.

The Hartman family had returned, and the six missionaries on the field voted. Five voted that I should return to the States for the surgery: I voted to have surgery in Brazil.

The following morning we left Xambre—leaving our belongings for the others to pack away in barrels; leaving our new Brazilian friends; leaving the country to which we had been called; leaving a work for which we had spent many years preparing; leaving it all—not knowing when, or if, we would ever return.

In Sao Paulo we obtained our exit papers, and boarded the plane— New York, our destination. Thunder rumbled and lightening flashed as we left the ground in 90-100 degree weather. We climbed above the storm and watched the lightening streaks below us. Here above the clouds the sun shone brightly, and we saw the beautiful silver lining. What we have heard, "...every cloud has a silver lining...," we were seeing with our own eyes. *Does each thing that happens in our lives have a reason—a silver lining? ... Why are we on our way back to the U.S.A.? ... Oh why, Lord?*

When we landed in New York the temperature registered minus-10 degrees. What a change. Our wee boys were shivering and we had nothing more to put around them.

We boarded another plane for Chicago where Uncle John and Aunt Ferne (Ummel) met us. It was so good to see them, crawl into their warm car, and head for Elkhart, Indiana. We had no home, or belongings, but we had a wonderful God and wonderful relatives—an uncle and aunt who came to Chicago to meet us with an invitation to stay in their home.

Immediately we inquired where we should seek medical help, and discovered an excellent urologist right there in Elkhart. Our little sons could stay with Uncle John's family during the time Jackie spent at the hospital with me.

Although we brought the X-rays from Brazil, Dr. Lundt wanted his own for comparison. He decided to do minor surgery rather than the major surgery recommended in Brazil. If necessary, he could do more extensive, or invasive, surgery later. Many people were praying for us.

Three men had already filled the other beds of the 4-bed ward to which I was assigned. Every day ministers and church leaders came in to visit and pray with us. They didn't have far to come as our District Office was located in Elkhart. My roommates were amazed at the stream of visitors, and the prayers they offered. One of the men said, "If you don't get well fast, none of us will." My hospital stay lasted only a few days with regular follow-up appointments in the doctor's office.

Within two months my ureter came down to the size that the doctor had hoped it would be in six months. Furthermore, he told me "there is no reason that you can't return to Brazil". He had corrected the defect with minor surgery.

He said my one (and only) kidney was twice the normal size and in excellent condition; my other kidney had probably "not functioned since, or shortly after, my birth"; and my "active lifestyle had kept things working." However, there had been a shortage of good drinking water in Xambre, and the time spent with language study had kept me less active than before going to Brazil. All of these things "contributed to this weakness showing up so soon in Brazil."

After being dismissed from the hospital, we left Uncle John's farm to visit Jackie's family in Ontario. They needed the assurance that all was well. During our stay in Canada, Aunt Ferne phoned to say their big barn had burned. We soon returned to Indiana to help our dear Aunt and Uncle who had been life-savers to us on so many occasions.

Our denomination is Mission-minded: thus our Mission is church supported. When new candidates are accepted by the Mission Board, their support is taken on *by faith*. The churches choose the missionaries (or projects) they wish to be responsible for, and *by faith* (in God to supply finances and answer prayer) accept the financial responsibility and the prayer support for the missionary, or missionary project. Definitely we believe our Mission is a Faith Mission.

As missionaries come home on furlough, they have an obligation to an assigned deputation schedule—going to churches and groups to present the challenge of Mission work on their particular field—and especially to the churches who have pledged to pray for them and to pay their support.

After the doctor pronounced me "doing well", we were asked to travel on deputation to the Mid-west Conference: Iowa, South Dakota, Nebraska, and Kansas. We had spent all our time in the Frontier pioneer work, and had taken many pictures: what a blessing. We left our boys on the farm with my mother—Grandma (Edith) Ummel—while we traveled three weeks giving nightly messages.

At this time we were unsure about our return to Brazil. Our hearts were there, and we had a strong desire to return. We asked the people of our churches to pray for the leading of God in our lives. We loved telling of the things we knew firsthand from the interior of Brazil, and had good meetings. The Lord blessed us as we ministered to our mid-western churches.

Time came for the Mission Board meeting—May 1957. Just one year previous we had given our Call and been accepted. So much had happened during the past year. We had grown so much in our faith in God. Now we faced a new anxiety—*would we be allowed to return to Brazil?*

After a time of waiting and suspense while the Board met in a private session, Brother Richard Reilly, Secretary of the Board, came out of the room and asked, "Are you ready for the news?" This only prolonged the suspense.

Then he smiled—Dick Reilly's entire face smiles when he smiles—and said, "Well, get ready ... you can go back in August and begin all over again ... and go to Language School."

Halleluiah – Praise the Lord!

We laughed and cried at the same time—God answered prayers—we were going back. In addition, another couple, Samuel and Eleanor Ross, had been accepted. They would be going in August also.

Again we said Good-byes to our families in Ontario and Indiana. The documents would be waiting for us at the Chicago Airport.

L-R: Stanley, Arlo Knouff, Herbert, Lois (Knouff), Richard, Jackie, Max, Phyllis, Mother, Robert, Joan, Art & Carol Hines, Fluella & Eldon

On arrival in Chicago no one could seem to find our passports until about ten minutes before boarding the plane. Found: on a desk under a telephone book.

Once again God intervened, and another confirmation that we were in His will.

Chapter 7

Return to Brazil—1957

The trip back by plane in 1957 was quite different than the 1956 trip by freighter: a contrast of 24 hours compared to 23 days. We didn't feel far away any more. Also we would be living in the large modern city of Campinas—a far cry from Xambre.

Jean Granitz and their two children had been in the U.S.A. from February to July of that same year. They experienced God's healing hand on little Lori. Their family had been reunited and rejoicing in it, and came to meet us on our return—August 15—my 32nd birthday. We soon rented a home and moved in. Our boys felt … *Home at Last.*

The Ross family arrived in Campinas, settled into their home, and enrolled in our class in Language School—beginning in September (1957). Language study had never been easy for me, but I was determined to learn, and studied almost all day and nearly every evening.

On the Frontier we had picked up enough language to do our own shopping and visit with our neighbors. However, most of the Frontiersmen could not read or write. We had picked up grammar and expressions that needed correction. In some ways this made it harder for us. Yet we enjoyed being able to communicate even in our *hill-billy* way of speaking. They advised that most missionaries are assigned regular mission work *after* a year of language study.

In the month of November two of our Mission leaders, Rev. Q.J. Everest and Rev. R.S. Reilly, President and Secretary of the Board respectively, visited our field. What a pleasure to see Bro. Everest who was not only the Board President, but also the man under whose preaching Jackie had been saved back in Ontario, Canada. It was a special pleasure for her to entertain him in our home here in Brazil.

During the time "Q.J." and "Dick" were with us, all four of our couples met with them in business meetings. We discussed many things and made plans for the future. One proposed plan asked the "Ummels to go to Xambre in 1958 on completion of Language School."

At that time it was difficult to submit to such a plan after all that had happened just one year previously. But through all the discussion, God gave us peace that He would work it out for us.

The schedule of the Language School allowed both parents to attend: fathers went in the forenoon; mothers in the afternoon. I admit it seemed more practical for the men than the ladies. In the morning I was more alert; I could catch either the streetcar or a bus; and because the Brazilians were very friendly, I could practice my Portuguese with them on their way to work.

After a full forenoon of concentrated study, I was tired. Our two small sons took their after-lunch nap, and I could rest with them while Jackie went to her classes. Almost daily the boys and I walked downtown—about a mile—to "meet mother" at the Post Office after her classes. Many times we left home early to visit the city park and walk through the "jungle" to see all the animals in cages. The boys always wanted to see the monkeys, and talk to the big parrots.

As a family we took *bonde* rides—a type of streetcar—out into the country, had picnics, climbed hills, and explored. The boys enjoyed hunting stones of different sizes, shapes, and colors.

On Christmas Day (1957) we took a train ride on the old wood-burning, narrow gauge train down through the mountains to Santos. What a difference from the previous year—now we could speak some Portuguese; felt secure and independent in our little home—just the four of us managing on our own. God had been so good to us, and now allowed us to enjoy a few days of relaxation at the beach.

We walked a lot that year for we had no car. In reality, it was a blessing as I got to know my two sons better. We walked all over our end of the city. Often we permitted the boys to run ahead of us, but *never* to cross any street until we caught up with them. Previously

I had been so busy working or studying that they had been in their mother's care most of the time. As we got farther into the mission work, my family became a real asset in going with me to services and make visits. Often they traveled with me as we went for supplies. As much as possible, we did everything together as a family unit.

In August of 1958 we graduated—received a certificate stating we had "passed through" the Language School, Escola de Portugues e Orientacao. Paul and Nila Mast, our 5th missionary couple, arrived in time to attend our graduation. They, too, helped us pack once again, and away we went—heading southwest to Xambre, Parana. Yes, back to the place of so many good, and yet many painful, memories—but without any anxiety. We had only Peace in our hearts, for God was directing us. He was with us and would protect us and our little family to which we would soon be adding another member.

The Mission had purchased a new Jeep, making this trip another new experience: driving the rough roads over which we had flown two years earlier. Brazil was building roads, but had very few good roads in 1958. For more than one-half the trip across the state of Sao Paulo we traveled on dirt or gravel roads. To make it worse, the other half was "under construction". Many times we had to wait on the road crews and road equipment, or take detours. At the time, the state of Parana had hard surface roads only within some of the city limits.

It's difficult to describe the roads of Parana or the interior roads of Brazil. Very simply—it's either clouds of dust or deep slippery mud. After only a small rainstorm, those roads of clay are as slippery as ice with a little gravel scattered only on the steepest hills. Many times we encountered from 10-150 trucks waiting on the hillsides for the roads to dry out enough for them to continue. During rainy weather every town, big or small, would have hundreds of trucks awaiting dried out roads in order to continue to their destination. Often a Jeep or small vehicle would make a new trail—sometimes into a field—to go around the big trucks. These trucks do not pull off of the road as it would be impossible to get back on the road again.

Almost all of the trucks traveling on the back roads are straight jobs with their weight on the drive wheels. Some have double axles with both axles pulling. Most of the back axles of the trucks will not drive—only carry the weight. These trucks usually have flat beds whose loads are covered with canvases. All the grain and coffee came sacked for hauling. Trucks heading east to the coast were heavily loaded with lumber, logs, and farm produce. Those going west carried food staples, farm produce, tiles for roof construction, plus other needs for the Frontier.

We saw many families headed west with their belongings. Anywhere from one to five families often rented a big truck to move all their earthly things. In this arrangement the families rode on top of the load, and were called *mudancas* (moving with everything). Some families who were a little better off had a horse, mule, or a cow in the corner of the truck along with their dogs, chickens, goats, and other animals. When a truck of this type stops, they set up camp by the side of the road and cook their meals on the spot.

Dry roads are another story. The red dust gets on everything. It coats all shrubs and trees along the roadside. Often you will see the powdery dust four to six inches deep covering the road with only the track bare where the wheels run. As vehicles travel, a cloud of dust is visible for almost a mile behind them. We welcome a side-wind to carry the dust away. Many times we placed a handkerchief over our nose in order to breath.

Usually the day after a rain is the best time to travel. It may be a little slippery when you get out of the track—but there is no dust. A little later when the trucks begin to move, there is a lot of congestion on the roads.

Brazil's first bridges were made of wood. They have a strong log framework, but only one vehicle crosses at a time. If a truck approaches and blasts his air horn—you wait. On these bridges the biggest vehicle automatically has the right of way. Also when they are headed up a hill, they will stay in the main track—you wait unless there is room for you to pass on the berm, or shoulder, of the road.

When approaching a curve on these narrow Frontier roads, each driver feels more secure when you blow your horn before rounding the curve of a narrow road. Although these roads had less traffic in the early days, it still was necessary from the very start to be a defensive driver.

Some of our Baptist friends from Language School had moved to Cianorte, Parana. They invited us to stop there on our way through. We pulled into their place late in the afternoon so dusty and dirty that they just stood there and laughed at us—our teeth and eyes shone white in the midst of the red dirt and dust. We asked them to take some pictures of us.

"our teeth and eyes shone white"
(Taken later, after Anita was born)

When these pictures reached our family in the homeland, they got more comments than the other pictures.

We arrived at our new home in Xambre with pets—a baby black kitten, Bitsy, who had traveled with us from our backyard in Campinas; and a black-and-white puppy—a gift from our Baptist friends.

Before our arrival to take over the work in Xambre, a beautiful big church had been constructed, and dedicated in June.

Putting finishing touches on the tower of Xambre Church
March 1962 Renovation

The Hartman family had moved on to Perola, and rented a home at a large sawmill nearby. Soon after their move, we took up residence in the Xambre parsonage.

Our very first night in Xambre we had charge of the mid-week service at the church. God helped us in these immediate responsibilities, and our year at Language School had really helped. But it seemed impossible to speak fluently. At least I tried my best, and the Brazilians had a lot of patience. Jackie played her accordion, and we depended heavily on religious film strips. Many of these films were available through CAVE, an interdenominational group working in Brazil. We showed the pictures and read the script by flashlight.

Each Sunday evening we showed these religious film strips in the church. Xambre had a big electric generator, but it broke down more than it functioned. We had to always be prepared to get along without it. So I adapted my projector to work off of the Jeep battery when we didn't have electricity at the church or one of our farm services. Without a theater or other activities in town, many people came just for the entertainment. In addition, they received the message of salvation.

Earl had many preaching points around Xambre that we maintained. Any night of the week we had 80-100 in attendance at these various places: one of these from the very beginning was **Fazenda Peroba**, the CSF farm.

In the first years the farm had a big turnover of workers. Shortly after someone became interested in Christianity, they moved on to another place. Although this farm seemed almost like Mission property because of the welcome we received, the church work developed slowly.

The Japanese farm, **Fazenda Ouro Verde**, about nine miles from Xambre became one of the best preaching points. During the time we lived in Xambre, Jackie had gone to the farm to assist an expectant mother with her delivery. This helped greatly in the friendly reception we received at this farm.

Fazenda Perigao also had become a good preaching point with its three worker *colonos* (villages). The farm was about the biggest farm in the area. In fact so many came to the services that we outgrew their largest home. In the cool weather they built a big bonfire around which we held our meetings. On several occasions my face became very warm in the glow of the fire while my back almost froze.

Several sawmills invited us to hold services. Many times a convert from one preaching point would move to another sawmill or farm. They would get permission from their new employer, or administrator, to have services in their new home. The man who invited us had the responsibility to invite his friends and neighbors, and so it went: many, many invitations and services being held each week.

A little later a family of Christians from **Fazenda Jardim** visited our church in Xambre, and invited us out for a visit. **Sr. Jose Jaco de Silva** and his wife, Sra. Alaide, had been members of the Presbyterian Church. They wanted their family of twelve children to be brought up under a Christian influence. Without a church of their denomination in the area, they invited us into their home for regular Bible studies. Soon their neighbors began coming. They put their simple living room table on the porch, and many gathered around on the grassy area in front of their home for singing and Bible study. As we continued going back on a week-night every other week, the group grew until seldom we had less than 100 in attendance at their home.

Later, one of these boys, **Edenias**, felt called to enter the ministry. After graduating from our Bible School in Maringa, he became one of our pastors and had a good ministry. Eventually, for a short period of time he became Superintendent of the National church.

Each pastor receives his own gifts and calling. In no way should we try to copy or follow others. We should not look down on anyone who is working differently. Some are evangelists; others, apostles. I Corinthians 12 speaks of the different gifts that God gives to us. I felt that God had called me to pastor especially to the *Heads of Families*. Then each father is to be the pastor of his own family, and then extend to his neighbors. In view of this, from the very start I had a wide open opportunity on the Frontier of Brazil where the men are still very much the head of the family.

Some of my earliest teachings pointed out to me that a Christian father must love his wife and have great respect for the partner that God had given him. Early in my ministry I noticed that if a man were saved, soon his entire family would follow him.

At times when the ladies made their decisions first, immediately I taught them to love and respect their husband and be submissive to him until he saw Christ through them. Some of these ladies went through hard times with difficulties and persecution. But generally their husbands also accepted Christ. Sometimes husband and wife came at the same time to accept Christ into their life and into their home.

Within a short time our ministry at the different preaching points became based around a family, or several families. Many times we went as a family to hold a service on a farm. We left around 1:00 or 2:00 p.m., and returned home around midnight. This gave time to visit the families on the farm before the evening service. I'd take my sons and go out to see their hogs, chickens, and other animals. Also I took a look at their coffee trees and other crops.

It's hard for me to realize why any farmer is not a Christian— farmers have to work so close to the power of God and in the will of God: God sends the rain, sunshine, wind, and other elements: the farmer must depend entirely on God. Some have asked why God sends the insects, frost, hail, wind, and other things: a frost has wiped out many crops. I answered ...*at times God has to show man who is in charge and all-powerful.*

My experiences in farming helped me to be sympathetic to their problems. How can a pastor, or fellow Christian, not have concern for the social or material welfare of others. A heart of compassion is one of the greatest needs of any Christian.

At times our host family would invite us to join them for the evening meal. We would visit in different homes in the after-noon, and be back in time for supper. Quite often the host would accompany me all afternoon, and we would return to his home just before dark.

Jackie always took an interest in the ladies and their children. She had many opportunities to give them information on better hygienic practices. Usually the children had an ailment—infections from cuts or insect bites—beside the many childhood diseases. She had very few idle moments as the many children and ladies gathered around her, and followed her from house to house. Generally she had her First Aid kit with her. She advised them on medications that could be used against the most common infections, and sometimes gave it to them.

Eye infections and the common colds were normal on the farms. Everyone is greeted with a handshake, if not a big hug or an *abraco*. It became a constant battle with our own children to avoid these infections. Although we taught them to wash their hands regularly, it is hard to keep their little hands out of their eyes, especially with so much dust. We always kept special eye drops with us for such occasions.

Time for the evening service on the farm came "when it gets dark." The farmers work according to the sun—very few of the workers had watches. The host family put on a feast for us. But we were hungry, too, after an afternoon of walking and visiting. In addition to beans and rice, they usually killed a chicken or rooster. Some of the children began to arrive at the (host) home before we finished our meal. At other times when we were without a meal invitation, we packed a picnic lunch and found a place near the jungle to enjoy our meal.

Jackie began playing her accordion in front of the house as the sign that the time for service had arrived. In a very short time the neighbors would begin coming—many just for the entertainment. Whether they sang or not, they enjoyed the music and knew I would be showing a religious film after I finished speaking.

Although the service lasted for more than an hour, they would still ask Jackie to play some more music. Sometimes they sang for another hour. After this, our new converts and the Christian men would begin to ask questions about the Bible.

The new converts had a real interest in the Bible. They used every spare minute to study their Bible and sing the new choruses and hymns. On rainy days with little inside work, some of them came together all day for studying and singing. So they always had many questions to ask regarding something from these (group) Bible discussions. At times like this I learned to appreciate my own Bible studies at the College and Seminary.

Usually I was able to answer their questions. If I didn't know the answer, I told them that I would study these passages at home using my commentary and cross references. Then at our next meeting I usually had an answer for them. These new Christians would quote my interpretation of Bible passages as pastors in the U.S.A. quoted commentaries. Continually, I asked God to give me correct explanations to pass along.

We never had a set arrival schedule for a farm service. Sometimes we stopped at some other farm or home along the way. At times we couldn't get there much before dark—the time for the service. Very seldom did we go home immediately after a service. By the time we arrived home, it was usually midnight.

I will never forget a service that we had at the Fazenda Ouro Verde farm, about a month following our return to Xambre. After the service ended, one man came over to the table where I sat, and said that he wanted to become a Christian. He was sincere, and soon had accepted Christ in sweet simple faith. In the light of the small kerosene lantern, he looked to be a poor withered up old man. Later, as I met **Sr. Joao (John) Chagas** in the daylight, I realized that he wasn't more than 40 years old, and had a family of five children.

In a short time his wife accepted our Lord as her Savior, and their children soon followed also. His mother and brother made their decision. Later, a young man who courted Sr. Joao's oldest daughter, Maria, stepped out for Christ. Sometime later, just before we came home on furlough, I had the privilege of performing my first wedding in Brazil—Amilton and Maria. Later in this book you will meet this young couple as we visit in northern Brazil, in the territory of Rondonia located in state of Mato Grosso.

Also on the Fazenda Ouro Verde farm, **Sr. Jose Cordeiro** accepted the Lord (during the ministry of Earl Hartman) only a short time before we returned. We held most of the services in Sr. Jose's home. Then one by one his family made decisions for Christ. Later as we had more responsibilities in taking over the entire area of Xambre and Perola, Sr. Jose became my lay pastor in Perola. His children were active in the church, and became leaders in our Young People's Group. The whole family sang in the choir.

Sr. Evaldo Pinho, another convert from the Ouro Verde farm, made his decision for Christ in an evening service about a year after we moved to Xambre. He immediately became interested in witnessing for Christ. Every time we met him—on the farm or at church—he always asked for "more Gospel tracts." He gave everyone he met on the road a tract and an invitation to the services: he handed out at least 100 tracts weekly. Often he sang choruses and hymns as he walked along the road, or while working in the fields.

Although he lived nine or ten miles from the Xambre church, he seldom missed a service, and came in for the midweek services. Every Sunday he came for Sunday school and stayed over to attend the evening service. Several other people would sometimes come with him. His family also became active in the church and Sunday school.

After about two years, Sr. Evaldo moved his family to a small farm within a mile of the church. They became more active in the church, and Sr. Evaldo began teaching the adult Sunday school class.

One day after he had done an excellent job of teaching the lesson, I asked him privately when he did his studying and preparation for teaching the class. He said that he started studying the next Sunday's lesson on his mile walk home after Sunday school. Our lesson books had devotional readings for every day of the week which always related to the next Sunday's lesson. These studies he said he used for daily family devotions in their home. So when the next Sunday came around, he only had to review for the lesson. Quickly I assured him that he had a good plan, and that he should keep up this practice.

This Christian man (Sr. Evaldo) had a real compassion for his neighbors, and in farming, a real gift at raising hogs. Almost all of his corn and *mandioca* (an edible root) he fed to them. When he butchered, most of his neighbors came for a piece of meat. His big trouble: he had very little left over to sell in the city, and the neighbors forgot to give back to him a piece of meat when they butchered.

I tried to show him that his family suffered while many of his neighbors had many more material possessions of this world than he owned. But he would say, "God understands and will repay me."

Sr. Evaldo lived on the main road where the chicken buyers came along regularly to purchase chickens and truck them to the larger cities to be resold. Sr. Evaldo started buying chickens from his neighbors to sell to the truckers as they passed his house. He always took tracts to distribute as he rounded up the chickens. In order to help some of the other poorer people, he gave them the same amount of money he received from the buyer, and sometimes more.

Sr. Evaldo wasn't in the chicken business very long, but he learned to know more of the people in the area. No matter what the circumstances were, he always gave a positive testimony for God. Usually he worked barefoot in the fields and carried his shoes to church, wearing them inside the church only. When the bow of his eye glasses broke, he tied that side to his ear with a string.

One morning sometime later, he was bringing the cows from the pasture to be milked, and his glasses fell out of his pocket. After searching, he found them only to discover that a cow had stepped on one lens and completely shattered it. Unable to buy another pair or repair it by Sunday, Sr. Evaldo wore them unashamedly in front of the church to teach his Sunday school lesson. Had this happened to me, I believe that I would have had too much pride to wear such glasses. But he was concerned only about his duty to teach his class — not his appearance.

Too often we are easily turned off because of the personal appearance of a speaker or leader, without hearing and understanding the message that God has given to them. Sr. Evaldo became one of our best church leaders. You will hear more of him later.

Sr. Ari de Mello, another big strong Brazilian, also lived on the Fazenda Ouro Verde farm. His transformed life in Christ began a few months before our arrival in Xambre, and during Earl Hartman's ministry. Jackie had helped his sister-in-law in childbirth two years earlier, and now Sr. Ari and his family attended almost all of the services held on the farm.

His story goes like this: One night on the way to the service Earl had seen a drunk sitting on the road. When he stopped, he realized it was Sr. Ari. There had been a Mass at the small Catholic chapel on the crossroads where the little country store-bar of Copacabana is located. Sr. Ari had been helping all day at the chapel and hadn't eaten any food since early morning. The priest had given each of the helpers a drink at the bar for their services. Sr. Ari said he often drank at this bar and other places in Brazil. But usually he did not drink on an empty stomach. He said in his stupor he couldn't speak, but knew almost everything that was said, or was going on. That night he also came to the service, and at the conclusion stumbled up to the front for prayer. God saved him in this condition, and he never had any desire to return to this former type of life.

Sr. Ari had moved to a small farm only about two miles from the church. When I took over the work in Xambre, Sr. Ari became one of my closest friends and a helper in the Brazilian church. He had a great interest in knowing the Bible and God's will for his life. Sr. Ari attended school only a few days in his life, but he had learned his "sounds". Since Portuguese is a phonetic language, he could sound the words out slowly. He perfected his reading by sounding out the letters as he read and studied the Bible.

I suggested that he study and read each verse several times until he could read a portion fluently. Soon he read so well that the people thought he had been reading all his life. He accompanied me to the services almost every night of the week. God led him to give his testimony in church as well as in the farm services.

His wife, Sra. Antonia, accepted salvation also. They had been married by a priest in another state, but never had a legal ceremony. Upon receipt of their birth certificates and other documents, we helped them legalize their relationship. Jackie and I served as witnesses. Later I had the privilege of baptizing both Sr. Ari and Sra. Antonia. At that time they had four children. Five more children were born to them—three of the five delivered by Jackie.

Soon the family moved next door to the Xambre church and became caretakers as well as workers in the church. Their children faithfully attended the Sunday school and the Children's Club that Jackie held for the children of Xambre. Their oldest daughter, Gerva, went on to attend the Bible Institute in Maringa. She graduated, and became a pastor's wife.

Sr. Valdemar Lacerda Neto and his wife, Sra. Algina, walked into the church one Sunday with their ten children, after finding temporary work on a small farm close to Xambre. We were glad to have this family attending our services. They came to us because there was not a church of their denomination in the area. They were Christians who had been active members of the Presbyterian Church in the state of Minas Gerais.

Our Fazenda Peroba (CSF) Church did not have a strong Christian family, and Don Granitz wanted to start a day school. Since Dona Algina was a teacher, Don hired her. The family soon moved to the Peroba farm, and Sr. Valdemar was given a nice section of coffee to farm with the help of his sons. This greatly pleased the family and also gave a great boost to the school and spiritual ministry at Fazenda Peroba.

These six families that we have cited—Sr. Jose Jaco De Silva, Sr. Joao Chagas, Sr. Jose Cordeiro, Sr. Evaldo Pinho, Sr. Ari de Mello, and Sr. Valdemar Lacerda Neto—became the nucleus of the church during our first (five-year) term. Other families attended also. Since each family had many children, we had a very active Sunday school and Young People's group. The ministry developed with a well-rounded program for all ages.

In addition to these families, a young Japanese fellow who worked in a store in Xambre—**Mario Miki**—began attending our services at Xambre. After service one evening he asked to stay behind to pray with me. He very sincerely made a decision to accept the Lord as his Savior, and became a firm Christian. Soon he became my helper in many ways. He went along with us to the farm services, and read the script for the religious films. Sr. Mario was baptized in the Xambre River at our first baptism service.

It was hard to watch him leave for Maringa to finish his high school studies. After graduation from Maringa Bible School, he continued college studies while holding a pastorate. Many years later when he became the first National President of our *Igreja Missionaria Unida do Brasil* (United Missionary Church of Brazil), I had the privilege—as Vice President—of being *his* "helper".

Jackie adds: *Later Pastor Mario became a professor of Bible, Theology, and Church History in two different Bible Schools, and is now (2007) continuing his work with the ministry of HCJB (Heralding*

111

Christ Jesus' Blessings) broadcasting from Quito, Ecuador. You will read a part of his extended ministry in later chapters.

Chapter 8

Reaching Families

Six months after our moving to Xambre, Earl Hartman and his family moved to Ribeirao Preto, Sao Paulo. Hartmans were the ideal couple to open any new work. In a short time they knew personally the leaders in the community and many business men in the city. Yet they had a great concern for the common laborers. By the end of their first term they had seen three churches constructed—Xambre, Perola, and Ribeirao Preto.

During the time Earl had charge of the Perola area, they had opened new preaching points from Perola on to the big sawmill on the Parana River—a distance of 40 miles. When another sawmill (or big farm) opened, the Hartmans were right there to welcome the newcomers.

As the Hartman family moved on, automatically we had almost twice as many preaching points. Consequently, we had to ask our Brazilian Christians to take over more responsibilities, but we still managed to get to each preaching point every two weeks.

In going to these many places, we found the families attended services even in rainy weather. Of course, if it rained heavily for a full day, there would be no use for us to go: the roads would be impassable. On some of these rainy days we just visited our key families. They needed encouragement.

Services at the Parana River sawmill usually had very good attendance. We learned the best time for that place was every full moon. In addition to the local workers, many Frontiersmen from the islands (in the River) could come with their motor boats and row boats. On a nice moonlit night we usually had more than 100 present. Usually a Jeep load of our Christians from Xambre went with us to help lead singing and give their testimonies.

The insects were terrible—always. Along the River we had more insects than at any farm service: the more light, the more insects. They flew in swarms around the light of our kerosene pressure lantern. Often we used only their small kerosene torches.

During certain seasons a type of hornet flew at night. Several times I casually brushed one of these hornets from my face—and was stung. As I reacted to the sting, the Brazilians had a great laugh. At the time I became disgusted because it really did hurt. Later I learned this is only how they react, but they really felt very sorry for me. About once a week I would swallow an insect while speaking, and I always had a glass of water close by to help wash it down.

These workers were very transitory. We didn't have a strong Christian man at this place to encourage others and to be a witness. Many had moved out to this particular Frontier leaving their families behind. Others were young men who wanted to make good money so they could get ahead—then move on, marry, and settle down at another place.

During these first years we had many decisions for Christ, but more of them moved away than the few who stayed. However years later we heard from other Brazilian pastors and missionaries who worked on the Parana River and the Mato Grosso Frontier, that they had met many people who at some time had attended the evangelical services at "the sawmill at Porto Byington on the Parana River."

Our main preaching points began by being centered on one or more Christian families. Services started in this way at the Byington sawmill on the Parana River and at the big Fazenda Perigao. Although some of our largest crowds were centered at these two places, from them we saw no visible evidence of church growth for our own denomination. They were transitory workers with only a few families among them.

At the same time the Pentecostal churches worked very hard at proselyting converts from other churches—especially from foreign mission groups such as ours. Even some of these church leaders said that many of their own leaders came from other churches—very true. We had good friendship with some of our converts that became lay leaders in several Pentecostal churches.

We left tracts with every adult at our services: usually at least one of their children can read. If not, they will ask a friend or neighbor to read it to them. Although we have seen no visible results in our church from some of these preaching points, we have done much sowing. God will reap the harvest through some of His other servants. The early preachers and colporteurs (Bible salesmen) of the last half century have helped open up Brazil for the churches of today. Very seldom have we encountered open opposition like the earlier ministries had.

Personally, we did not try to change their culture, but just teach and preach the Bible. When a missionary starts a new work, even the small things can become traditions. We wanted to fit into their culture.

One of the first things we realized was that the farm and home services should start after sunset. We didn't set a definite hour for the service to start. Their whole livelihood rested in their farm work, and many times they needed to work until dark. We tried to be patient and not start too early. When we saw people a great distance away walking in, we often just began singing without any testimonies, children's stories, films, or speaking, until they all arrived. We learned to go a slower pace. It was best for us, and this created a friendlier, informal, and more relaxed atmosphere.

Our church stood on the edge of the jungle. Many of the men walked from one to five miles to attend services. Many of these families had a dog to accompany them—a protection as they walked through the jungle on those trails. We soon learned we should also permit the dogs to come into the church. They slept contentedly under the seat of their owner. Tied outside, they barked at every person or other dog that passed the church. Seldom did a dog bother the service.

One time in a home service I accidently stepped on the foot of a dog that was sleeping under the table. When the dog howled, the crowd just laughed. We went right on with the service.

A few years later we had a big tent campaign in Perola—one of many different tent campaigns. This campaign happened to be in one of the more civilized areas where the dogs generally never go to church. At almost every meeting a dog would break loose, or jump the fence, and come into the tent during the service. One of our ushers kept running up and down the aisles trying to catch the dog or chase it out. He caused far more distraction than the dogs. One time we stopped the meeting because he had become the center of attention.

A missionary has a different responsibility than a pastor. The missionary goes to teach the Bible and Biblical methods to the people, and help them to stand firm on Christian principles—not the customs of foreigners. If he (or she) doesn't do this, something is wrong. When starting a new work, of course, in many situations the missionary also needs to be a pastor. Having practical pastoral experience in the culture will help greatly in the training of national pastors. We (our UMS Mission) didn't want to transplant an American church in Brazil through a Bible Training program.

When there is famine and starvation in an area, they need food, and it may have to be given to them. If over a period of time, they aren't trained in how to increase their own food production and how to care for themselves, we really haven't helped them at all. If left untrained, the next year their food shortage would be greater: the population grows and they haven't solved their own problem.

The spiritual ministry is similar in many ways. The Christian way of life is more than just a revival campaign, and more new commitments to Christ: they need spiritual food, counsel, and guidance. Each individual, family, and church, must be trained to stand on their own feet: to depend on God—not the missionary or the Mission Society. This must be done from the very beginning.

Most church groups in Brazil do not give away Bibles, but sold them. When Bibles are purchased, they are much more likely to be read and appreciated. In some places they are sold at less than cost in order for the poorer people to own a Bible. Brazilian Christians often give a Bible (or song book) to a friend or relative as a gift.

It is also a custom that each person owns his own hymnal. Most churches do not furnish hymnals. The people carry both their Bible and their hymnal to the services. In a short time most Brazilian

Christians have the well-known hymns and choruses memorized. We encourage and appreciate this custom.

The Brazilians were getting along before our arrival. When we leave—if we have done our work—they should be getting along much better. Our task is to help them understand and express more of the Love of God. We were more than a Bible teacher or preacher: we expressed our concern and compassion for them.

A missionary nurse or doctor sees many needs and hopes to not only help them physically, but teach and train them how to avoid and prevent suffering and sicknesses. This cannot be accomplished over night, but over a period of time as the individuals find confidence in the missionary who wants to help them improve their way of living in their own culture.

Our family brought a great blessing to my ministry. When I preached of family unity, the people had to see the "unity". We raised our family on the Frontier: God protected us. Jackie was in the early stages of pregnancy for our daughter Anita when we returned to Xambre from Language School—September 1958. However, we arranged things to be able to attend the Annual Meeting of missionaries and workers in Campinas held in the early spring. Very soon after the Meetings adjourned, our little Brazilian daughter, Anita, was born—March 10, 1959—in the Maternity Hospital at Campinas.

Anita was only a few days old when we brought her—a healthy baby—back to Xambre. God had His hand on her. Because Jackie nursed her, she went to all of the services. Baby Anita came into contact with all of the diseases the other children had—and caught some of these diseases, too. As some children got sick, some died. They asked Jackie how she took care of our infant daughter. Only then were they ready to ask and seek more sanitary methods of caring for their children.

Most Brazilian mothers nurse their babies. This custom bothered me in a church service. Whenever the babe gets hungry the mother is ready to nurse, and most of the time one or another of the mothers would be nursing her child. Some nurse until the child is a toddler—two or three years of age. Very few of these mothers took any precaution not to expose her entire breast. Every time a mother began to nurse, I noticed that I had no more eye contact with the men. They were watching these ladies who seemed to have no modesty in nursing a child.

I asked Jackie to nurse Anita in the services, too. At first it was difficult for her. However, when Jackie nursed our daughter she placed a clean diaper completely over her shoulder covering Anita's head and the nursing activity. In a short time every husband had his wife doing the same thing, and I never had to say a word in public.

In those early years we had difficulty maintaining a good milk supply for the family until I purchased a cow of our own. Then we had plenty of milk for our own family, and to supply our national worker.

Soon some of the farmers from Fazenda Peroba, and others living close by, noticed that I milked more milk from my one cow than most of them milked from several cows. They wanted to know how I took care of my cow. Also over the years I have been able to give advice and counsel in agronomy (economics of crop production/management) as well. However we were not there for that purpose. We were there to help them in spiritual, physical, and material ways of life. Daily we asked God for His guidance in these matters.

The Brazilians on the Frontier were very conservative. In their testimonies most of the Christians would state that God had saved them from smoking, drinking, and football (soccer). The main soccer games were played on Sunday, making it almost impossible for a person to be at a game and also attend the church services. Many fights occurred at every game. Most of the stadiums in Brazil had been built so the spectators could not get onto the field to enter into these fights. Some of the officials even came and left the games in an old army tank. Therefore when the scriptures say ...*abstain from all evil...,* the people consider these sports "evil".

I did not push the subject, but remained neutral on the issue. Most of our youth worked so hard at making an existence, that soccer games didn't affect our Frontier churches too much. Later however, when our youth went to the Annual Youth Conference in Maringa, soccer did become an issue within our National church.

At this time I clearly testified that I had played football in college, and had won letters at two different colleges. Also I explained that I would rather have my sons kicking a soccer ball in my front or back yard than to have them walking the streets, not knowing where they were going.

But with all I said concerning my attitude toward the issue, most of the conservative Christians in those early years would not permit their children to play. I told the youth that they should obey their parents even when it involved soccer.

Because of this issue a good number of our converts became easy prey for the Pentecostal church's proselyting. Even some converts who had been baptized in our church left in those early days. Being given a position in the new church, of course, helped their pride and kept them satisfied a while.

God blesses us even in our weaknesses: music and singing is not my gift. Right from the beginning I always asked one of our Brazilian Christians to lead the singing. This meant that our new Christians have been very active in the services. Many times after the Bible study, I turned the alter call over to one of our pastors or lay leaders. In many ways this became an asset in the ministry: it made the service a Brazilian service, and prepared them to hold their own services. Jackie played her accordion in almost every service. The Brazilians appreciated her music just as much as my Bible teaching. The Brazilians who had guitars played along with the accordion.

Most hymns and entire hymnals have been taken to Brazil by various churches, and simply translated into Portuguese. The Pentecostal churches have many hymns that are more of a Bible story put to music with many verses. These hymns tell the story of David, Moses, and other people from the Bible. As the leader goes along singing, he may add more verses. In the past few years many scriptures have been set to music, and are accepted very well by the Brazilians.

Accordingly, we have started our services with about a half hour of just singing these scriptures put to music. The people go from one verse to another with individuals—one person after another—calling out their favorite verses. A few times they became so enthused with singing hymns and scriptures, no time remained to preach or teach from the Bible.

The Byington Company had a great interest in medical care. One of the first houses built in Xambre was a home for the doctor. However, during our first term there, the town was left without a doctor more often than it had a doctor.

Sr. Aldo, the Company administrator, recommended that some of the expectant mothers call my wife who was a registered nurse. The only other women that worked as midwives were involved in witchcraft. They also used unhygienic practices. After Jackie saw one of these midwives in practice, she couldn't turn down the opportunities to help when they called.

We purchased a stethoscope, blood pressure cuff, other simple medical supplies, and a First-Aid kit. In fact, she took over my briefcase for her midwife satchel.

The Lord helped in every situation. Usually she didn't want to accept any case without some previous check-ups. But many times there were no opportunities for pre-partum checks. I would take her in the Jeep. If any complication arose, the Jeep would be available to take them to a hospital in Umuarama.

Through these opportunities we got into many homes, and began to more fully understand their problems. At times, the labor period lasted for hours—even overnight. I sat many long hours with the men and neighbors waiting around a little campfire on the outside—or inside—of their home. In the wintertime, they actually made a small fire on the dirt floor in the middle of the living room using dry wood that didn't make much smoke. At times some of the children slept in the same room. The ladies gathered around the crude stove in the kitchen where there were enough cracks in the walls for the smoke to easily escape. At least these fires helped warm us a little.

It was very interesting to listen to their stories and experiences. Although we never made too many converts through this ministry, we had many close friends. Many of Jackie's patients lived in Catholic homes, and the homes of the best merchants in Xambre. We believed a Christian should have compassion for all. Many newborn baby girls were named *Elizabeth*—Jackie's name in Brazil.

The Frontier roads do get bad, and especially without the use of gravel. They only clear a trail through the forest; take out the big stumps with a bulldozer; bring in road graders to level off the "trail"; and call it a road. With a good rainfall, a lot of erosion happens. The normal rainfall is about 75 inches per year. One time we had eight inches within 24 hours: the streams were mud-colored.

One night in our second year at Xambre, at about mid-night we heard clapping—the Brazilian custom of knocking—in front of our home. Standing there in the rain was a man from a nearby farm. With my flashlight in my hand, I called him to come onto our covered porch. His wife was having trouble in childbirth and he said he needed to take her to Umuarama where, by this time, several doctors resided.

I explained to him that it had been raining for two days and no vehicle had been through to Umuarama. He said he knew this, and the town Jeep-taxi would not try to go, but told him that "Pastor Ricardo, the American, always gets through when nobody else could get through...." I tried my best to keep our vehicle tuned up and in the best shape possible; sprayed my whole ignition system with water repellant so it wouldn't drown out easily; and prayed all the way that God would help me get through.

After I took Jackie to check the lady, we knew that she had to get to the hospital. At this time we had a young hired girl as a helper in the home. She could take care of our two sleeping boys, and we took off well after midnight on the 30 kilometer (18.75 mile) drive in a light rain. The roads were very soft from two days of hard rain; and every hillside, very slippery and muddy. I drove into each soft spot with the Jeep in four-wheel drive and low gear range. I did not want my motor to cut out.

One long upgrade was almost a kilometer in length, and it looked like a riverbed. Although at that moment the rain had almost stopped, a solid stream of water gushed down the hill from the previous downpour. The front bumper of the Jeep pushed slush and mud almost the entire way up that hill. In second gear in the low gear range, the motor worked at full capacity. I knew that if we stopped, there would be no way to get out by ourselves. Needless to say, both Jackie and I were praying out loud to God, and every few minutes the lady had a labor pain.

As we pulled up in front of the hospital we were still praising God for getting us through. The lady had a hard delivery. Medical attention was needed absolutely, and the Lord had helped us get there.

I've seen Jeeps stuck in the mud with only a few inches of the tires sticking out above the mud and water. But this was one of my worst trips through the mud. The circumstances for the trip and nervous tension made it a difficult and memorable trip.

Both Jackie and I felt that Jackie's first responsibility was to be at my side in the evangelical services. She took her cases with this reservation in mind. However, there were times when it became necessary to attend to our Christians, including overnight stays at the hospital.

Another time, a Japanese family who owned the local coffee mill and was a grain buyer had contacted Jackie to help in the delivery of their baby. We had left our house for a service when they came to call for Jackie's help. When they didn't find us at home, they contacted a local midwife. We arrived home about midnight both tired and hungry after the long service. With our big kerosene lantern glowing, we sat down for a snack before going to bed. Our house stood on a hill where everybody in Xambre could see that we were home.

The Japanese family saw our light and came to ask Jackie for help. His wife was having long hard labor, and had become so weak that she almost had stopped trying to give birth. After Jackie examined her and confirmed that everything was in good order, the lady relaxed, and the baby arrived in a few minutes.

Sam Ross, the superintendent of our Mission in Brazil, made periodic visits to each station, and at times reached his destination by plane and bus before his telegram.

One evening Sam arrived at our home shortly after we left for a service. When he found the house locked, he went over to the church and slept on a bench.

That night we arrived home late and very tired, and were getting ready for bed when we heard clapping on our front porch. Jackie had several delivery cases that were "close up", but she didn't think tonight's timing seemed right. In English she said, "Oh, I hope it isn't another baby case tonight. I'm so tired!"

Sam yelled back, "This is a different kind of case," and we warmly welcomed him inside. We had a good visit while Jackie fried some eggs for a snack.

The next day he accompanied us as Jackie did have a baby case—another difficult one. We were glad Sam was there to help us pray.

Another Japanese girl came to Jackie for her delivery. Since this was her first baby, and by all indications it would be a large one, Jackie felt led to refuse the responsibility. She offered to accompany the young lady to the hospital in Umuarama.

God really had guided Jackie in this decision as it also was a very difficult case. Jackie stayed with her in the hospital, helping the doctor and midwife to care for her. The baby died the following day. This was a difficult experience for Jackie who, at the time, was in the middle of her own pregnancy before Anita was born.

The next day when I went back to get Jackie in Umuarama, I drove on another 30 kilometers (18.75 miles) to buy bottled gas and fresh vegetables: Cruzeiro de Oeste which recently had become a branch store from Maringa was the closest place to get bottled gas for our cook stove. While on this trip, we had a heavy downpour of rain making our trip home very muddy and slippery.

It is easier to control a Jeep from slipping sideway on the road while going uphill than when going downhill. The wheels hit a big rut in the road, and the next thing I knew it had slipped into a big washout at the side of the road. The weight of the vehicle no longer was on the wheels: they were just spinning.

After the jolt, Jackie asked if everything was alright as she looked the boys over. I said, "No," for I had bumped my head very hard on the electric windshield wiper, and blood ran down my forehead from a deep cut.

When stuck like this, Jackie usually drove while I pushed. If others were with us, they helped push. Today two men came along. I asked them to help us push. They helped a little, and then left saying it was "impossible to get it out without another Jeep." Jackie didn't want me to help as it only caused my head to bleed more.

Looking the situation over, I told her we would try again. I put my back against the front of the Jeep fender with my feet along the side of the road against the bank. It came out. But the force I used to do this caused the blood to spurt from the wound.

But—after hearing about Jackie's experience with the young lady and her baby, I wasn't in the mood to return to Umuarama. I had more confidence in my wife than the doctor, and continued to hold a small hand towel to my forehead as Jackie drove on back to Xambre. She was able to borrow a suture needle and thread from the local drug store, and soon had three stitches in my forehead—her first experience with stitches. She did it on our back porch as the last daylight faded away. The cut kept seeping blood. Every time I got up from the cot to help start the lantern or to do other odd jobs, it bled more.

This happened on a Wednesday night: our regular scheduled night for Bible study and prayer meeting. It had rained again and only our dear faithful brother, Sr. Ari de Mello came for the meeting. Jackie called him into our front room for prayer instead of going to the church. God performed a miracle for us—and the bleeding stopped: Praise the Lord.

The people at Fazenda Peroba took more interest in the Gospel after Sr. Valdemar took charge of the spiritual ministry there. He conducted a Bible study the week we were not scheduled for a service. Then the farm truck began to bring their group every Sunday into Xambre for the Sunday school service. The truck also picked up many people from Fazenda Ouro Verde who walked out to the main road to ride along. These farm people helped to nearly fill the Xambre church each Sunday.

Xambre always had ladies and children, but not too many men. The men came occasionally for special services, but never became firm Christians. If we showed pictures on a Sunday evening, the service had good attendance, but never as large as the services on the farms. So the church people were greatly pleased when the truck arrived with the farm groups, and gave them a hearty welcome.

The baptismal services and Christian programs became our special occasions. We arranged for Fazenda Ouro Verde and Fazenda Jardim to send in their trucks, too. They helped fill the church to capacity with about 200 in attendance.

The baptisms were quite eventful. We drove through the town on the way to the River, and many from the city followed us to witness the service. The candidates dressed in white for the occasion: the men wore white shirts and trousers; the ladies, white gowns. Usually we baptized a dozen or so at each of these service. The candidates usually invited all their friends and relatives. Consequently very few—less than one-half the group gathered by the River—knew Christ as their Savior. The short message, singing, and testimonies of the candidates along with their baptism, made an impressive service. We had baptism services as often as we had the candidates—at least once a year.

Another festive occasion came in December: our Christmas program. Jackie would give out plays or readings at the different preaching points, putting one person in charge at each location to help the children and young people with their assignments. Then every 15 days she would rehearse with them to see how they were doing. When the time came for the program, each group presented their part in the combined program.

Our third Christmas in Xambre (including the first one when we couldn't speak the language) Jackie had more than 60 people participating. What a busy day: the day Sr. Paulo's wife died.

She had been ill for a long time, and it was imperative that she be buried immediately—the same day. We promised that we would be there. We figured we would have time for a short funeral and burial, and get back in time for lunch and the Christmas program which began at 2:00 p.m. However, this didn't happen.

When we arrived at Sr. Paulo's little shack, we discovered the wooden casket had not arrived. In fact, the casket had arrived—too short—and it had been sent back to be rebuilt. The young boy who took the measurement to the carpenter, cut off some of the string which was meant to determine the length of the casket—yes, unbelievable, but it happened.

When the box—which it really was—finally arrived, we had the service. Then the men carried it through a jungle trail, onto the main road, and to the cemetery. Jackie took our two sons with her in the Jeep and drove around by the road. When she caught up with us near the cemetery, she said she watched the bottom of the box bounce up and down, fearing it might break at any moment. As I helped carry the box, I felt the same way and kept praying that God would hold it together. Finally we arrived at the grave site, had a prayer, and the burial. Everyone threw dirt in the hole and on the casket.

I arrived home completely soaked with perspiration, enjoyed a quick shower, and immediately went to the packed church where they were singing as they waited for the program to start. All went well with the program. But we were a tired family at the end of that Christmas Sunday.

God blessed our New Year service each year. These services usually started just a little later than a regular service, and carried over the midnight hour into the New Year.

Around 11:00 p.m. we had a coffee break, followed by a communion service (partaking of the sacraments), and entered the New Year in a prayer time around the altar.

God also blessed our other services in Xambre. Another time when the church was filled to capacity, a big rain and windstorm blew in from the west with a big black cloud from horizon to horizon as far as we could see. The Xambre church stood on the top of a hill where one can see over the entire countryside. The people became fearful and afraid. So we had a special prayer asking God for His protection over us and His church building.

I had hardly finished the prayer when the cloud divided and went around the church. Everyone watching it felt the Presence of God. For years the Christians talked of this occasion.

The year 1961 had the first good coffee harvest in the Xambre area. Many of the families on Fazenda Ouro Verde harvested enough of their share to buy a small farm of their own: most of our Christian families purchased land close to Xambre. So the last part of our first (5-year) term became the best year for our Xambre church. Now we had some landowners, and their tithes really helped to improve the financial situation in addition to the good assistance they gave in all of the services. Also, many of these Christians were willing to go along with us to the farm services on week nights.

Every day more families moved into the area. Our Christians helped some of the newcomers—many were distant relatives—to obtain work. Before long some of these new pioneers dedicated their lives to Christ. I needed more help, so God called Sr. Ari de Mello to be my lay pastor and caretaker at Xambre. We also purchased a small rubber-tire cart and a good mare to pull it. With this Sr. Ari could take his family to hold services at other places in the area: the mare could be used to help him on his small farm.

Then Sr. Jose Cordeiro purchased a small farm close to Perola. He lived in the house built behind the church for a lay pastor and caretaker. To have Sr. Jose's assistance was a *God-send,* for at this time we also had weekly classes in studying the Bible and the administration of churches: his coming surely was of God.

Just the year before this, Don Granitz and his family moved to Fazenda Peroba in preparation for the first coffee harvest. Don became a real asset to the spiritual work. His wife, Jean, had a great compassion for the needy and sick who lived on the CSF farm. Many times Jackie accompanied her in the homes of the workers. Jean's friends and relatives would have been greatly shocked to see some of the situations where Jean went to help the poor and needy.

As we worked with this couple a very close fellowship developed between us. I had first met Don as the outstanding Conference quarterback on the Taylor University football team; I was playing in the center of the 5-man defensive line for Manchester College. Now we were working on the same team with God as our Coach.

In September 1959 the Granitz family went home on their first furlough, and the oversight of Fazenda Peroba became my assignment. Although I had the assistance of a Brazilian farm manager and two lay pastors, the load became very heavy. Having grown up on a dairy farm I thought I had to be up at daybreak either in my study or at work. With a service scheduled for almost every night of the week, we seldom got to bed before midnight. I was almost exhausted, and we had come into contact with hepatitis in the area.

The first Sunday in January (1960), we had another big baptismal service at the River in Xambre—such a blessing to baptize so many converts. Although exhausted, the cool water helped me regain strength for the next candidate. I thought I could rest on Monday and be back on my feet soon.

"...the cool water helped me regain my strength..."
January 1960 Baptism

About daylight a day or so later, the farm manager clapped at our front door. While taking a sick man to the hospital in Umuarama, the farm truck had stopped on the road. Without a mechanic in Xambre at the time, I gathered my few tools together and went to help: carburetor trouble. We didn't get the truck going until about one o'clock in the afternoon. I had been out in the hot sun for several hours.

Arriving home, I told Jackie that I wasn't hungry—just very tired and thirsty—and stretched out on the living room sofa. When she took my temperature it was 104 degrees, and my eyes were yellow already. Jackie recognized the hepatitis and knew I needed immediate medical care. It had started to rain and rained hard all night.

In the morning she drove through the mud to Umuarama to charter a plane for Maringa where I could get help. A young Bible School student went with her to help in case she would get stuck. As they left Xambre the Jeep-taxi driver stopped her and said the road was absolutely impassable. Jackie asked the driver to please go for her. He said that in no way would he return to Umuarama until the roads were dry again. With the rain continuing to fall, she drove on to get help. Only God helped them get safely through to Maringa and back to Xambre that day.

We arranged for one of our sons to stay with a family; the other one to remain in our home with the Bible School student; and Anita would go with us. We were in readiness when the clouds cleared and the small plane buzzed our house. Jackie, our little Anita, and I drove to the airport and soon we were in the sky above Xambre.

In Maringa (January 8, 1960) the blood tests verified hepatitis. They wanted me to stay awhile at the hospital. But because my wife was a nurse, the doctor consented to let me go home. He gave us prescriptions, and carefully wrote out the instructions for the medication and medical care, knowing that Jackie would care for me in every detail.

As we flew back home the next day we thanked and praised God that we didn't need to be flown back to the U.S.A. as in the previous situation with the kidney problem.

Jackie—the best nurse I could have had—took good care of me. The first week I slept almost 22 hours each day. She only awakened me for shots and meals. She also protected me from the many visitors that came to see me by setting a time limit for each visit: a custom they had never heard of here in the interior of Brazil.

The local church leaders helped Jackie with the services during my time of convalescence. Jackie went to the scheduled meetings to drive the Jeep and play her accordion—a real load and responsibility for her. However, faithful Christians who traveled with her helped when she was stuck in the mud, and took charge of the testimonies and Bible study in the services. This helped to lighten her load.

After four weeks I felt much better, but the doctor *demanded* that I rest two more weeks to be completely well before taking over my responsibilities. One time I wrote the farm payroll from my bed with the farm manager right there to help me.

Going through this illness taught me that when I got tired, I should stop and rest. I usually rested in the afternoon before an evening service. When many people are ill, they do not get a thorough rest, and the weakness from the sickness affects their lives for years. Within six months I had no symptoms of the illness— Praise God!

The Maringa Bible Institute began in March 1962. Three boys from our area went to prepare for the ministry—the Japanese youth, Mario Miki; Edenias, son of Sr. Jose Jaco de Silva; and Cleber, son of Sr. Valdemar Neto. In the next few years about four more entered the student body.

Chapter 9

Furlough Time—1962

A t the end of April 1962 we began our journey home for our first furlough. We came home a few months early in our fifth year because we were expecting another addition to our family: the plane would not carry anyone during their last 30 days of pregnancy.

On the last Sunday we had a big day—the church didn't want us to go until absolutely necessary. It was hard to leave our new children in Christ. We had packed all of our personal possessions in barrels and boxes; put them in safe storage until our return; the tickets had been purchased ahead of time; our passports were in order; and our packed suitcases loaded into the Jeep before going to church for our last service. We needed to be in Umuarama to board the plane at 1:30 in the afternoon.

Everyone came to church early as they knew there would be no time to visit after the service. Three of the Fazendas arranged trucks for their Christian groups to come to the farewell service. With all the seats filled, many had to stand around the sides of the church, and some stood in the entry way. It was a long service.

Since we had a baptismal service on the previous Sunday, today these candidates were accepted officially as members. Also we dedicated to the Lord several new babies.

My farewell message took longer than I planned as many were so young in the faith, and I knew they needed a lot of love, patience, and guidance to withstand the many attacks of Satan. After they presented me with a lovely fountain pen, they sang *'Til We Meet Again.*

With only time to embrace and say Goodbye to our lay pastors and a few of the church leaders, we immediately got into the Jeep and drove directly to the airport. Many tears were shed, and because of my own tears I could hardly see to drive: *Could it be that we were really leaving them all, and wouldn't see them next Sunday as usual?*

We were excited and happy with the anticipation of again seeing our friends and loved ones in the U.S.A. and Canada, and another joy because of the new arrival to be born into our family in June. Even so, our hearts ached to leave our young Christians behind with no regular pastor to guide them for another six months. Odd as it may seem, it was harder to leave Xambre that day than it was to leave our homeland family and friends in 1956.

A Baptist friend met us at the Umuarama airport and took the Jeep to his home until a fellow missionary could pick it up the following week.

We thought we had a direct flight to Londrina. After about 20 minutes into the flight, they announced that we would be stopping in Maringa. What a surprise.

Our fellow missionaries discovered that our flight had a 10 minute stop, and came out to say their farewells. With eyes still tear-stained from leaving Xambre, it seemed good to have a last *Goodbye* with our co-workers: we would be meeting many of their parents and friends within a few days.

The flight home on the Braniff plane was the most beautiful International flight I ever had. The plane was one of the last four-motored planes before going to jets. It flew low enough to see the scenery—the beautiful rolling countryside of western Brazil. After the Frontier we saw jungle—hour upon hour—actually flying around the mountain peaks and not over them. One time, we flew around an old snow covered volcano. I snapped some pictures looking down into the mouth of the volcano.

Our first stop—Lima, Peru. Soon darkness kept us from seeing more of the beautiful majestic Andes Mountains.

The plane arrived late in Miami. We were rushed through customs; dashed, what seemed to be almost a mile to reach our connecting flight: we watched it leave.

Then we found we could get a flight direct to Chicago that would arrive before our scheduled flight. A phone call informed our family of our new arrival time just before they left home.

My two brothers and mother met us in Chicago. We stopped for lunch at one of those restaurants built over the Expressway. Cars went under us in all four lanes on both sides of the median.

Our seven-year-old Ted asked my brother Eldon, "Where are they all going?"

Eldon—amazed that the question should be asked—couldn't answer. He didn't realize little Ted probably had not seen that many cars in all the years he lived in the interior of Brazil.

Every missionary faces things like this upon their return home. Everyone is so busy continually, and going everywhere: *Is this busy life really God's will?*

Then soon the missionaries themselves become just as busy with their deputation schedule, and other things.

A couple days after our return the ladies of our Indiana District were holding their Women's Rally. They invited Jackie and me to be present at this meeting, but only to give them our "greetings from Brazil".

We had not been in a church to hear singing in English for nearly five years. The emotional impact was so great on Jackie that as she stood up to say a simple greeting, she began to cry and tremble. She could not continue.

Only those who have gone through such an experience know the feeling: *Yes, it is good to be home ... but yet so out of place and lonesome... our home and loved ones were in Brazil.*

While we visited our family in Canada, Jackie gave birth to Michael Lynn—June 5, 1962—at the hospital in Meaford, Ontario, Canada. This gave us two American sons, a Brazilian daughter, and a Canadian son. Two months later we returned to Indiana, where we made our home for the year of our deputation.

Speaking on deputation always worried me. But the Lord had blessed our first term so much that it became a privilege to share the spiritual blessing received on the Field in Brazil.

In our denomination, the missionaries on furlough attempt to raise the support for that year for the Foreign Mission budget. We went to the summer Family Camp Meetings at Kitchener, Ontario; Weeping Water, Nebraska; and Elkhart, Indiana. In the fall, winter, and spring months, my schedule as a Missionary Convention speaker took me to churches in the Michigan, Ohio, Nebraska, Indiana, and Ontario conferences of the United Missionary Church (today known as the Missionary Church). Some of our church leaders seemed greatly surprised the way God helped me to minister in these Conventions. We Praise Him.

We sailed once again for Brazil on June 6, 1963—our children 10, 8, 4, and 1 year of age—a most enjoyable trip of only 16 days on a semi-passenger/semi-freight ship. The boys enjoyed the swimming pool while the passengers doted on Anita. Our one-year-old cutie, Michael—a little fat rolly-polly toddler—became the favorite of our stewardess. So Mom and Dad had a great trip and a relaxed vacation.

Chapter 10

Back Home in Brazil—1963

Arriving back to a land that we knew, and a language we knew, was much different than our 1st and 2nd arrivals. We took over the work in Perola, Parana.

Sam Ross had moved to Xambre in the fall of 1962. Many new farms had started since we left for our furlough home. Thousands of new pioneers had come into the area with another truck load arriving every few hours both day and night.

I borrowed the CSF farm truck to haul our furniture and things from Xambre to Perola. The two older boys rode on the back of the truck singing Portuguese choruses at the top of their voices. They remembered going to the services with the Brazilians who always sang all the way to and from services—our boys were happy, and back in their beloved country.

In Perola a nice home had been built for us by the Mission, and we had only a five minute walk across town from the house to the church. Here in the interior a home can be built for less money than the cost of renting a home for one term. We had the privilege of doing our own landscaping, and plantings of trees, grass, hedges, and flowers.

Our fellow missionaries in Campinas gave us a German shepherd pup—a great playmate for Anita and baby Michael. Rick and Ted soon had to go away (with other missionary children) to GreenAcre Boarding School in Maringa.

When we visited Perola for the first time seven years earlier, only three homes had been built. Now in the immediate area of the city, five large sawmills were operating to supply lumber for building materials. Perola had developed into a nice town, and we saw the need to concentrate here in building a local church. Invitations to hold services came from many homes, each sawmill, and several of the nearby farms.

After getting settled and visiting our church members, we wanted to set up a good public address (PA) system. All of the frontier towns depend heavily on the PA systems to announce news, sales in various stores, and political speakers. Churches had them, too. In Xambre a 30 watt system could be heard—depending upon the wind—within a radius of two to three miles. We wanted the same for Perola, if possible.

Since our church was very small (5 x 8 meters), we needed to install a tall pole on which to mount the big horns. The horns would be run by a battery or a small generator—no electricity yet in Perola. With a setup like this, we could announce our special services and play music over the town before and after each service. It worked.

In 1964 Norman Charles and his family assumed the supervision of Fazenda Peroba. They did a good job administrating the farm, and had an outstanding spiritual ministry. Norm and his wife Betty had compassion for the people and always were ready to help out to the minute detail. Their five children also ministered along with them. God brought this family from a Mennonite background— Pennsylvania Mennonite Church—to assist in our mission work in Brazil.

After their experience (in Pennsylvania) of being filled with the Holy Spirit, their church asked them to leave. God had blessed Norm and Betty with a healing ministry and a greater love for people. Their lives manifested the fruit of the Spirit. When God called them, they came to Brazil without a Bible School or college education. The church work on the farm and in that community grew abundantly. For nearly eight years they blessed our churches with their ministry.

During the year 1965 a beautiful church went up on Fazenda Peroba. Soon it became the largest Sunday school and church group of our Mission. The Ross family from Xambre, the Charles family, and our family had good fellowship. Our church groups also came together for special occasions: Christmases, Baptisms, Spiritual Retreats, and more.

Co-Laborers also entered our area. They had two big farms: Fazenda Santa Fe, about halfway between Xambre and Perola; and Fazenda Ouro Verde, about 30 kilometers west of Perola. Founded by Rev. Maurice Sand, their main purpose was to get laymen from the U.S.A. to come as missionaries and work in a cooperative program with any, or all, evangelical churches in Brazil. Their venture in developing coffee farms extended to raising cattle. George and Faith Pidcoke stopped in our home in Perola. A good friendship developed with this group and grew over the years. Having fellowship with American Christians from time to time became enjoyable.

During our first term we were kept very busy and didn't have much relationship with them. However at the times when we did meet, our fellowship was good. They had a busy and difficult job in getting their project started—an orphanage, too.

Bethany Fellowship—a branch of Bethany Missionary Fellowship in Minneapolis, Minnesota—purchased a portion of the Fazenda Ouro Verde with the purpose of starting an independent Bible School in that area. Their *Work Program* provided their students with an opportunity to be a part of the Fellowship, and enabled the participating students to attend Bible School without needing finances to continue their schooling.

Bethany's founder, Rev. Ted Hegre, enjoyed a close friendship with Rev. Sand. This led Bethany to work in a close relationship with Co-Laborers. We learned to know Bethany's missionaries very well as they came into the area, and maintained an excellent relationship with them.

The work in Perola continued to grow with an exciting youth group and regular services until our small church became completely filled. Two small covered buildings were built to provide more Sunday school classes; and yet another class met in the living room of our deacon-caretaker's home.

At Christmas—always a special time of year—the Santa Fe group put on a full Christmas Story drama using horses, a donkey, soldiers, and other things to create a real-live play. Around 30-40 people acted in it. They taped portions to be played over the PA system.

Just before the service the "soldiers" rode their horses through the town. We followed the procession in the pickup truck announcing the service, and playing part of the taped program over the PA system. The procession led the group onto the church grounds where they presented the play.

About half of the church area had been roped off for the stage, and the audience—more than a thousand people—had to stand away from the church grounds and even into the street. The next year, with the permission of the town authorities, we roped off part of the central plaza and put on the same program. More than twice the number of people came to watch.

In July 1964 we and some of the students felt led to have three big evangelistic tent campaigns: Perola (City); Fazenda Peroba (CSF farm); and Casa Branca—a big sawmill and village at a cross-road between Xambre, Perola, and Fazenda Peroba. Each of the three places held one week of meetings. The tent belonged to our Mission and had been used in Campinas, Sao Paulo, and other cities in Brazil. We filled the tent to capacity many times. At least two boys—switching off—stayed with the tent at all times. The setup varied a little at each place.

Our Bible School students were on winter vacation (with opposite seasons in the southern hemisphere) and available to help. Five of the students stayed with us in our home during this time, and at least two stayed in the tent every night. We were responsible for their meals and personal needs.

The meetings greatly blessed our work in Perola. The tent was filled to capacity almost every night. Our greatest blessing was watching these five young men in action—four were from the area. They all felt *at home* with the people. Each student had a different assignment each night: they really complimented one another and did a great job.

The Christian family who helped us to arrange and plan the meetings at the Casa Branca sawmill also allowed us to hook up our lights to their generator. What a relief not to worry about our small old generator. We always kept our kerosene lantern going in case the generator cut out. With no other attraction in the area, many attended each night.

Jackie played the accordion. She and one of the girls from Perola sang using some of the fellows in the background for harmony: they made a very good musical group. Very few people here had a church background, and didn't enter into the singing very much. We had many decisions each night. With no church at Casa Branca, the new converts were immediately proselytized by the Pentecostal churches of the village.

Then soon after the meetings ended, our host family moved on to another sawmill. Although we witnessed very little visible evidence of these decisions in our Perola church, our people were greatly blessed by helping in the services. Again: we are God's servants, and He knows the real results.

The tent campaign at Fazenda Peroba was very successful. Since the farm had a big generator, I didn't have the responsibility to keep my generator going. Don Granitz, dean of our Bible School in Maringa at that time, came to the services and helped us greatly during this campaign. Our Christians on the farm also helped in both singing in the spirit, and the devotional programs—leaving a great impact on each visitor that came to the meetings.

These tent campaigns were a great blessing, and had a terrific impact on our Bible School students. Their teachers reported these students entered into their studies the next semester with an entirely different attitude. We rejoice in the spiritual blessings that God gave us during those three weeks of meetings.

Chapter 11

Expanding the Work

Our Bible School in Maringa grew. The next year they needed another teacher. We knew that Sam Ross and his family would be leaving Xambre in January 1965, so Sam could fill that position as a teacher.

This decision meant that again we would assume the responsibility for the work in Xambre. With the Perola church filled to capacity we knew there should be an immediate new church constructed in Perola. Although we didn't have too many adult men in the church, we had a very good Young People's group—more than 20 teenagers in attendance many times. We prayed much about this. The church families were ready to work together in a building project—all wanted a new larger church.

We broke ground on August 15, 1964 with 20 men who came from Xambre and Perola to dig the foundation. Bricks already had been delivered, and the next day the foundation began. No small job. We didn't have electricity, and all the water had to be pulled up from a deep—100 foot—well with a hand-winch rope. It took three or four big strong boys just to pull up the water and carry it to the mortar box. Two carpenters had been contracted to be paid by the day, and we could put as many volunteer workers on the job as necessary.

In a few days one of the carpenters walked out on the job, and I went out to visit Bethany Fellowship. They promised to send in two missionaries to help with the framework. Neil Tyson and Dave Rennick came with a generator and electrical powered circular saws. Within a week the entire framework was up—10 x 15 meters (approx. 33 x 50 feet) that would seat comfortably about 250 people.

At least six volunteer workers came every day. They nailed each big truss together on the ground and put it up in one piece. When finished, our two sons, Rick and Ted, had fun painting the ceiling of the church. Three months from the day we started, we dedicated the building. God blessed and protected us each day of construction.

The Perola Church

On dedication day, November 10, 1964, the Perola Church was filled to capacity with more than 300 attending. The Xambre and Fazenda Peroba groups also drove in for this occasion. We were glad to announce during the service that there were no bills outstanding on the construction. However we were without benches, and had borrowed benches from the mission tent and other places. But at this service the people pledged money to buy enough benches to fill the church.

The Choir on Dedication Day

A few months later Dr. Kenneth Geiger, International President of our denomination, visited us. It was an extraordinary privilege to have him in our home and church. During his stay, he wanted to visit in some homes of the Brazilians in the area.

While in one of our very poorest homes on a small farm, the worker called me aside to give me the money that he had pledged for a bench. He had finished harvesting a crop of soybeans and had his bench money. After we left, Brother Geiger asked me if I had loaned this man some money, and I explained about the church benches.

Also while Dr. Geiger was staying in our home, we ran out of bottle gas. Because of the muddy roads, no gas was available in town. So I made a crude stove in the backyard with a few bricks and the top of a steel barrel—embarrassing for me, but he could see how God helped us by supplying our needs in a variety of circumstances.

The kerosene lamps used in the Perola church were replaced when we found gas lights that could be hooked up to our tanks of bottle gas. The lights worked very well when the pressure was up in the tank. So about every month I would connect a new bottle, and take the old one home to finish using it up on our cooking stove. At about this same time, I put up a gas light in our home.

Then after living in Perola for almost a year and a half, we were able to service our home with electricity. The mission had purchased a generator for Xambre, but the motor didn't hold up. When a 10 horsepower diesel motor came up for sale in Perola, I bought it and used the generator from Xambre: Sam Ross had moved to Maringa where they had electricity. The generator also helped to charge batteries for the PA systems.

God blessed the church in Perola. Many times our Sunday school attendance was more than 100; and the Sunday evening attendance, even larger. Our Mission kept records on attendance, and someone always had to count.

During our inspirational singing one Sunday evening, as usual I began counting the people. God spoke to me saying my job was not to count the people, but to preach the message given by Him. From that time on, I had someone else do the counting.

We had lots of transitory people: many of the day workers moved from one job to another: outsiders came in and bought many of the small farms around Perola: the earlier pioneers then purchased other land west of here to begin all over again.

One sawmill was shut down and sold. During the interval of being shut down, we had four families move away from the church within one week. In order to hold our own at the church, we continually had to have new converts and decisions for Christ.

One year we had many fires in the state of Parana due to the very dry winter months—May to September in the southern hemisphere. Along with the drought we also had a light frost which killed many of the crops. The workers on the farms used fire to burn off the land so it would be ready to plant again: they had no machinery to work the soil except their big hoes. The fire got out of control on most farms, even burning through much of the remaining virgin forests in all of western Parana.

The first time the fire went through the underbrush, it killed much of the ground level foliage. When this died down, another fire passed through. In many places the second and third fires felled many of the dead and hollow trees. We had to cancel some of our services because of fallen trees that we could not get around.

Clearing the Roadway

The smoke became so thick that we couldn't see a block away. At midday the sun shone no brighter than the full moon on a clear night and looked like an orange ball of fire.

A few homes burned, but nobody really knew how much damage had been done. We didn't hear of any deaths in our area from the fire. But this was not true in other parts of the state. The rains were a real blessing that year. It took several rains to really clean up and purify the air.

When Sam Ross and his family moved to Maringa in January 1965, we took over the Xambre church area in addition to the area of Perola. The Brazilian Christians continued to help with the services, visitation, and other things, or I couldn't have pastored the two churches.

Three of the Xambre families transferred to the Pentecostal church because it was more conservative and legalistic. A much greater contrast existed in those days between the teachings of the churches: the men had to wear a jacket and tie to services; for the ladies—no slack suits, short skirts, sleeveless blouses or dresses, jewelry, or cutting of the hair. Although this other group seemed to require rules and regulations, they always remained very friendly to us even after having been effective in proselyting.

Our western churches also were quite conservative, and the Pentecostal influences strong. Several times our fellow missionaries used puppets in telling Bible stories, and one time a Christian magician visited our churches. We had good attendance for the special meetings, but afterwards it nearly split our church—some did leave. Those who left were very legalistic and conservative in the interpretation of scriptures, using. Galatians 1:7-9: *Evidently some people are throwing you into confusion and are trying to pervert the Gospel of Christ. But even if we or an angel from heaven should preach a gospel other than the one we preach to you, let him be eternally condemned! As we have already said, so now I say again: If anybody is preaching to you a gospel other than what you accept, let him be eternally condemned!*

This became the main scripture passage for the basis of their thinking. In the Portuguese language these scriptures appear even stronger against *any other way of preaching the gospel* than it appears in the English versions.

However, those who had a real experience with the Lord—wanting to live for Him and manifesting the fruits of the Spirit—weren't as tempted to leave our church with its Biblical teaching.

Spiritism and witchcraft left a great influence on Brazil. Many of our Christians had been saved out of these group practices, and did not want to have anything to do with things that were questionable, deceiving, or had the appearance of witchcraft or magic. Many of the people had seen—and walked on—red hot coals on St. John's day, June 23.

On this day a large group of people gather to watch men walk on—and not be burned by—the red hot coals. Within these false groups many of the gifts are manifested as recorded in 1 Corinthians 12. Because of fear or curiosity, many people attend but they do not do it in love as emphasized in 1 Corinthians 13.

Knowing this and having seen all of this in their background, I never felt led to do anything in my teaching, or in an object lesson, that could appear to be deceptive or questionable.

Fazenda Jardim had a fairly good coffee harvest in 1965. Sr. Jose Jaco de Silva and his family also had a good harvest. They purchased a small farm close to Xambre. Later they sold it and moved to Umuarama, the commercial center of western Parana. We were invited to begin having services at their new home, and the attendance grew until soon their entire front lawn was filled with people.

A few months later I happened to be in Umuarama one afternoon doing some shopping. I stayed over for the evening service, and heard that the Byington Land Company had begun to sell lots in that area—and only a few blocks from where we were holding our services.

In order to obtain a lot for the church, I purchased it in my name—a nice corner lot in the Vila (working class area) of Umuarama. Later, when they were ready to build, I transferred the lot from my name to the church.

A building, 6 x 9.5 meters (20 x 32 feet), was constructed on the back of the lot with the intent of making it the future parsonage. A division on the back part of the building would provide a place for a young couple to live—a lay pastor or caretaker. Later the church would be constructed on the front part of this corner lot—the side which faced the other street.

One of Sr. Jose Jaco's daughters who had been very active in the Xambre church, and her husband, soon became the main lay workers here in Umuarama. The local group took care of the Sunday services, and any Bible studies they cared to hold. Wednesday night's midweek prayer meeting became our part of the schedule.

Since Umuarama had become the commercial center, we went early in the day each Wednesday and did our shopping in the morning, visiting in the afternoon, then stayed over for the midweek evening service.

Our Xambre schedule: Saturday night and Sunday morning. Then they began having home services on Sunday evenings in addition to the other services throughout the week. Sr. Ari had developed into an excellent lay pastor, and Sr. Evaldo, our deacon, very capably assisted him with the services. Several other laymen cooperated very well with these two lay leaders.

At this time Perola became our strongest work. We had Sunday school in the afternoon, a very good evening service, and the midweek service on Tuesday evening.

Each of these three churches for which I was responsible— Umuarama, Xambre, and Perola—had a PA system prior to bottle gas or electricity. I put a generator on our Jeep station wagon, and carried an extra battery in a box behind the back seat. In this way I always had a charged battery to leave with a church, and an extra one being charged as I drove between the churches.

The Lord helped me in every service. Before each service I needed much prayer, study of the Word, and meditation. I could use the same message at the times when I was not preaching or teaching to the same people. However, the message always had to be adapted to each particular group with illustrations varying according to circumstances. Because these people did not have the privilege of much education, the messages had to be very practical and applicable to their situations. Sometimes I only needed to prepare two different messages and a Bible study each week.

I meditated on my presentations as I drove along the roads. I felt God very near, helping and guiding me along the way. By using the same message a couple times in home services, it would be well prepared for my Sunday message.

The Bible studies seemed the easiest, yet more challenging to me as a continued study. These different groups could also continue to follow the study as they prepared for each following week.

God helped me adjust to each situation and circumstances as they varied from time to time. In case of a heavy or prolonged rain, very few would be present at the meeting. A simple Bible study along with the singing of well known choruses and a few hymns met their need. At other times someone might have a question, or a problem they wished to discuss. Where they needed help, we were free to meet their need with the Word of God.

At times we had joint services with the groups that I pastored. These usually were held in Xambre since the church was adequate in size and more centrally located. For the New Year's service, Christmas, Easter, Baptisms, Retreats, and other special services, we rented trucks and buses to bring the people together. This always filled any church to capacity with a time of spiritual refreshing for everybody.

A few times the group came to Perola. Again this packed the church as many local people who didn't come to church regularly, came for such an occasion. Several times the Fazenda Peroba church came by truck and their VW van. Each guest group usually brought along special music, and at times we had guest speakers.

Jackie was a great companion in our ministry. She listened sympathetically to their personal situations. Many of the ladies came to her revealing family problems—both spiritual and material. Before leaving a home, she usually knew of the family's existing problem(s). The Lord gave her the gift of discernment and compassion.

At times the situation would be a very personal family problem in which I never wanted to take the disciplinary place of the father. I felt the father—not the pastor or church board—is the one to correct his own children. However, if after much counseling he couldn't do it, it might become necessary to bring it before the church leaders. The Lord helped us in every situation. Some were complex and others very simple.

The last two terms on the Field we had a Volks Wagon station wagon. One time when we stopped for a short visit at a home, I tried to start the motor—it wouldn't start. I opened the *lid* and shone the flashlight on the motor. The first thing that the beam hit was the wire between the distributor and coil—it had pulled out of the coil. Within 15 seconds it was back in place with the *lid* closed. Undoubtedly some boy was hiding in the dark to see what would happen, as the wire was very unlikely to have come out by itself.

Motors need regular tune-ups, especially VW motors. Brazil has some very good mechanics. Over the years they have been able to keep many of the old cars running. Parts are often expensive, but labor here was much less expensive than in the U.S.A. Most of the mechanics tuned the motors by ear, because they did not have the electronic equipment. They do a good job and tell you to "come back if you're not satisfied."

Many times over the years when I have taken my vehicle to the mechanic, I've told them just what to do. Several times it was to advance or retard the distributor a little. Most of the mechanics in our area think that I really understood the whole thing, and have gone out of their way to help me keep our vehicles tuned up and running well. I never studied mechanics, only watched and learned from them in their shops.

These shops were my contacts with the world outside of our church family. I talked to them about many things and often talked about Christ, giving my testimony of God's latest blessings on our work, and in our family.

For the same reason I preferred the barbershop to Jackie trimming my hair. In the shop I can hear the latest news in town, and get acquainted with more of the men in the area. Likewise, Jackie went to the beauty shops to visit with the more educated women, and made contacts with ladies who would never attend an evangelical church.

A Jeep-taxi driver lived close the church. His house stood on the back side of the same block of our church. Although he only came on special occasions, his wife was one of the ladies who attended and only had to open the gate on the back of their lot to enter the church lot.

The church in Perola became a very active church with their "special occasion" services which brought in many visitors. The PA system regularly made announcements over the entire city and area, and thousands of tracts had been handed out over the years. Many in those days would tell others they were "members of the Missionary Church." What they really meant was that the few times they had gone to church in the past year, they came to our church. But at least they knew that we had a church and the evangelical message was preached there.

Each year our Mission had a Youth Convention on Memorial Day, and always on the weekend including the last few days of October and the first day of November. Sometimes we had difficulty getting over the roads. But each year was a great blessing.

In 1965 the farm truck took the group from our three western churches to the Youth Convention. The truck had a flat bed with sides about a meter (39.3 in.) high. They made benches by fitting a board into the framework of the side of the truck and attached one or two legs to support the weight of the passengers—six or eight persons to a bench—no backs on these benches.

They built a low wooden framework over the bed of the truck to support a large canvas. The canvas opened in the front for air to pass through with a flap that could be tied shut in case of rain or cold weather.

You guessed it. It rained all night before the trip. I began questioning whether we should—or could—make the trip. But as we waited in Xambre in the early morning hours, we heard the sound of singing. Soon the farm truck appeared with the youth from Fazenda Peroba. Norm and Betty Charles were with them.

The truck had on its heavy tire chains, with many big hoes and shovels tied up under the truck bed. Our youth climbed aboard. As customary, we had prayer before continuing on to Maringa, and they joined together in singing praises to God as our little caravan traveled along: I followed behind the truck in the Willys station wagon.

Most of the youth had been up long before sunrise getting ready to meet the truck at the Xambre church. Each person brought their own lunch for the trip. However, the group had been preparing for this trip for weeks, and the quizzing team studied for months preparing for the big Bible quiz. We had three quiz teams on the truck—one from each church. When they were not singing, they threw quiz questions at each other like darts.

As we passed through each settlement in the villages and towns, the youth tossed tracts to the people as they sang choruses and hymns. Within a few minutes every paper would be picked up.

It continued to rain. We had a long slow trip with many *pushes* to the truck. The farther we went and the longer we drove in the rain, the worse the road became. Because of the rain we didn't encounter too many trucks on the road. But the rain made the mud so slippery that, at times, we had to have two or more people at each side of the front fenders to keep from sliding off the crown of the road. The others pushed from behind.

At first we got on and off the truck very carefully. We didn't want to get too muddy or bring that red clay mud back into the truck. But after awhile everyone just jumped off the back of the truck. Some of the boys slipped and fell—unintentionally—in the mud, actually sliding on their backs. When they climbed back on the truck, others sitting near them became muddy, too. By the end of the trip everyone was completely covered with mud.

It began to get dark, and we still had the worst part of the trip ahead—over the hills and mountains between the Ivai River and Maringa. As we turned on our headlights the rain which seemed to have let up a little, began again.

Norm is a very good and cautious driver. But now we prayed out loud as we went up and down the mountains—more dangerous on the downgrade: chains do not hold vehicles from sliding sideways, and brakes can hardly be used as there is less steering control. The vehicle followed the ruts and fortunately, the ruts usually were in the middle of the road.

One time the truck nearly slid off a very steep cliff. We were going downhill and around a sharp curve when the truck slid sideways. The back of the truck actually hung out over open space. We prayed—Norm, too. Norm stepped on the gas and the chains dug in pulling us right back on the road. A shout of Praise rose up to God from the back of the truck.

Finally we were only a few miles from Maringa: it was still dark. Everyone became excited because our trip was near its end. Then suddenly, we couldn't move. We were bogged down in mud more than a foot deep and two big trucks, heavily loaded, sat crossway in the road ahead of us. They blocked our truck. The Willys station wagon that I drove made it into the coffee field, around the big trucks, and out again.

I took our Brazilian evangelist and a converted nun who had been helping us in some of our services, and went on into Maringa for help while Norm, Betty, Jackie, and all our young people stayed behind with the truck. They were not exactly comfortable for the night, but later admitted they even slept awhile due to exhaustion.

"...we were all muddy..."

As the morning sun crept over the horizon, I arrived back at the truck with two VW buses belonging to our Maringa mission. Everyone piled in—bags, baggage, and mud. Soon we turned into the driveway of the Maringa Bible School.

It had taken us 24 hours to travel 150 miles. Of course, all the other church groups had arrived the evening before. But all of their vehicles had come on blacktop roads, and many of them much more than 150 miles.

They were just awaking and, along with the Bible School students and missionaries, gave us a grand welcome. The showers stalls were kept busy for a time. Finally everyone was ready for breakfast and the morning service. Our youth were prayed up and expecting to see miracles.

During the morning service on the second day, the Holy Spirit fell or descended on the entire group. Within a few seconds the altar was filled. Some went into other classrooms to pray. Many knelt right where they were sitting. What an experience!

I don't think any missionary or young person had ever seen anything like it. Also I don't think one person left without finding Christ as their Savior—others found a deeper experience with Christ.

The dinner buzzer rang.

Word immediately went to hold off dinner for awhile. Everyone wanted to stay under the anointing of the Holy Spirit. Later we were dismissed to go to dinner, or stay, as each person felt led by the Lord. Some never ate their noon meal: many restitutions and confessions were made, and continued to be made, during the rest of the Convention.

The afternoon session began late, and started with personal testimonies. While the Testimony and Praise session progressed, the Convention leaders got together and rescheduled the remaining sessions. Nobody had expected anything like the Lord gave us.

This year the farewells after the Convention were prolonged more than usual as many friendships had been made—binding them together in the Spirit.

Youth attending the Convention

The road had dried from the hot sun and the road graders already had been at work. We made the trip home in very little dust. Within about eight hours each one of us walked into our own home again. What a contrast to the previous trip.

After a Convention such as this, the youth generally take charge of the Sunday evening service. They give their testimonies and teach their home churches the new songs and choruses that they had learned. The blessing this year was almost as good as the Convention itself. Each parent glowed with happiness, gratitude, and thankfulness to God to hear their own son or daughter give their testimony. Consequently, every year the entire church family looks forward to these special Retreats for our youth.

Every year we had these meetings in Maringa. We never could plan on road conditions, but we always got through one way or another. One other trip took us 19 hours. We arrived there nearly as muddy as this time. However, this particular trip was the worst trip to date.

Getting through to our regular services is not easy at times either, and upkeep on the vehicles has been high. But the people have been very sympathetic under these conditions, and when they see the interest that we have in them, they are even more open to the Gospel. We become so inspired—personally—with the spiritual victories that we soon forget about the discouraging road conditions. Others also get stuck on the road, too, and we are ready to help them.

During our second term we drove a Jeep station wagon. It very comfortably carried more people to help in the various services. As more vehicles used the roads, bad spots soon developed with deep waterholes after a bad rain—which can come at any time of the year. During these early years only 4-wheel-drive vehicles and the big trucks could consistently get through. Many times we helped others out of the mud so we could get through.

On one occasion a VW car traveled through our area. The driver cautiously went through a big waterhole. To avoid the deeper water, he had gone to the side of the road, but found the edge soft, and got stuck. Then it began to rain much harder.

As I approached, he waved me down. The water was rising with the motor already partially under water. He asked me to pull him out. As he was soaked from the hard rain, I didn't see the need for both of us to get drenched. So I handed him a chain and asked him to hook up his car to the back of mine. With the 4-wheel-drive and low range, it didn't take long to pull out the light-weight VW car. In a short time his motor could have been ruined. I pulled him another quarter mile before the motor started.

In 1965 the sawmill owner brought the first car into our area—a 1960 model 4-door Chevrolet. He also had a Jeep, and planned on using the car when the roads were good. But a sudden rain can change the roads in a few minutes, making it hard to tell the depth of a muddy waterhole. The big trucks wallowing through the waterholes soon leave some big ruts or larger holes right in the middle of the road. For these reasons I usually try to go around a waterhole—or right on the edge—with my lighter vehicle.

One day as I returned from Xambre, I encountered this Chevrolet sitting in the deepest spot of a waterhole with water halfway up the door. I backed up my vehicle to the car, took off my shoes and socks, rolled my pant legs above my knees, got out, and hooked my chain to his automobile. As I pulled him out, water ran out of all four doors. Again, the motor didn't start right away.

Earlier this man very reluctantly permitted us to hold services at his sawmill: he had many workers. But after this incident, every time I met him—in front of everyone—he called me his "pastor". As far as I know he never became a Christian, but as a good friend, he continued to allow us to hold services at his sawmill.

Our vehicle also got stuck on the road the day a fellow missionary family went with us to a service at Fazenda Peroba. It must have been a Sunday service—I had on a white shirt and tie. As we went through a big waterhole, the motor got wet but didn't quit until we were through the deepest water.

I took off my shoes and rolled up my pant legs before working on the motor. As I opened the hood, I could hardly see the motor because of the steam and mud. The whole electrical system and plugs were completely coated with mud. I rolled up my shirt sleeves and stood on the bumper to dry out the plugs, wiring, and anything else that needed to be dried. My coworker jumped out and took a picture of me at this task. (*Sorry, we couldn't locate this picture.*) On arriving home, I sprayed the entire electrical system with a water repellant brought from the States. This helped greatly.

Another time when returning from Xambre we noticed our neighbor—the Jeep-taxi driver—driving his Jeep ahead of us. As we encountered another Jeep from Perola coming toward us, our friend ran into the tall bank of dirt along the side of the road. His Jeep turned over on its side. I opened the canvas on the back of the Jeep and helped him out. He had been drinking, but the accident quickly brought him back to his senses.

In a very short time a crowd gathered. The gas began to run out of the tank so I said, "Let's set it up on its wheels. We are all strong men," and it didn't take long to bring it to an upright position.

Because of the sandy road, the Jeep wasn't hurt very much. The taxi driver began to tell everyone that I was his pastor, physically patting me on the back.

This accident happened almost in front of the crossroads and bar of Copacabana. His vision had been impaired from drinking. He claimed he had seen three Jeeps coming at him instead of one, and "had to get out of their way."

Everyone laughed when he told the story. Afterward he drove on home to Perola.

We were not without incidents either: there was the time when our headlights went out, and we traveled several miles on a very dark, dark night.

Again—one Sunday evening we had a service in Perola and the station wagon was filled with people from Xambre who wanted to go along and help in the service. We were traveling about 40 mph when a front wheel broke off. Immediately I had no control of the vehicle and no brakes: the brake line broke, too.

When the front corner dropped to the ground, the vehicle pulled to the right and we hit the bank along the road. The car had almost stopped, but the bank of dirt was nearly three feet high, toppling the car over on the left side.

Many screamed, and bodies piled up on one another. With about four people on top of me, I had a difficult time opening the passenger door and getting out. Soon I had the rear door open, and everyone piled out.

One lady hit the windshield and had a cut on her forehead that bled. The others were bruised a little, but no one seriously hurt. Again we praised God for His protection.

On examination of the Jeep station wagon, we found the housing on the front had broken. A week or so previously we had gone over some very bad roads with deep ruts. Undoubtedly the housing had cracked at that time, and took this opportunity to fall apart.

The next car to come along was Don Granitz, our fellow missionary from Fazenda Peroba. They "just felt inspired" to go that particular night to visit our church in Perola. How God worked this out!

Chapter 12

Helpers in the Ministry

In November 1966 the Bible School in Maringa graduated its first class of students. Two of these young men came to help us in the west. I had carried the heavy load of pastoring the Xambre, Perola, and Umuarama churches knowing these young men would soon be coming as young pastors to take over some of my responsibilities.

Mario Miki—the young man from Xambre, and one of these first graduates—felt led of God to take over the work in Perola.

Before graduation Edenias de Silva had dropped out of Bible School to continue his secular studies in Umuarama for a year. His parents, Sr. Jose Jaco de Silva and Sra. Alaide, had moved to Umuarama, and Edenias became a real asset to me as pastor of the church. During his experience with the church, however, God confirmed to him that he needed to continue his studies in Maringa to become a pastor.

When Edenias returned to Maringa to study, another first graduate of the Bible School—Elcy—came to take over the work in Umuarama.

We then moved back to Xambre to pastor there, and continued to be available to help these two new young pastors.

Our church in Xambre was no longer the same church it had been about four years earlier. A frost had hit the area in July and August of 1965. This was the first of the big frosts. One farmer had been offered $5,000 for his small coffee farm. After the frost he couldn't have sold it for $2,000. Their entire economy—except sawmills—was based on coffee.

The hard frost had not killed the roots. But the trees had to be cut off at ground level to sprout again. The farmers had continued to plant corn, beans, and rice between the rows of coffee on which to exist until harvest. A small coffee harvest could come in about two to four years. However, the trees would take five or six years for maturity to produce the larger crops.

The economy of the area had affected the church greatly, and became the beginning of the exodus from Xambre. Some of the people—most of them day workers or share-croppers—had just started their own farm. Fazenda Perigao and Fazenda Jardim, two of the big farms where we held regular services, were the first to put their land into pasture and raise cattle.

Sr. Jose Jaco de Silva and his family had been among the first families to move from the area. They became the nucleus of the new work in Umuarama. Many other families who regularly attended our church and farm services also moved. We had no way of communication to follow them to their new location. Some families couldn't keep track of their own relatives. Many came to us in an attempt to locate their loved ones who had moved on with the Frontier. The result: without a church, most of those who left were unable to stay within our denomination. Many became very faithful to other churches.

Because Brazil is so large and almost every city has some very good spiritual churches, our Christians fit in well and became a blessing to the local churches in the areas where they moved. We have done a lot of traveling over the years as we attempted to keep in contact with them the best that we could, and give them encouragement.

Each time we traveled through an area or city where people had moved, we stopped for a visit. Some of these trips—appearing later in the book—took us into the state of Mato Grosso, and on farther up into the Amazon Basin area.

Several big Land Companies advertised *Land for Sale* in other parts of Brazil. One big company from Londrina began to invite people up to the territory of Rondonia. In fact, they operated an agency in Perola, and had several big buses that made regular trips for people to visit this northern Frontier and "see for yourself."

Sr. Sebastiao who attended our farm church became the first person from our Sunday school group to purchase land and move into the area of Rondonia. He had a family of eleven children. Several of the older siblings had already married and had children of their own. Soon he moved his entire family north. Then the families of his sons- and daughters-in-law began moving north.

When we moved to Xambre we took our personal generator and motor along. We hooked it up to furnish power and lights to the Xambre church. This, along with our family living there, helped boost the morale of the church.

Then our term in Brazil changed from five to four years, so we had to think and prepare for our furlough in July of 1967. We felt led of the Lord not to launch out into starting or continuing the many preaching points which we originally had in our ministry: our church families and leaders needed spiritual food.

Several Christian families from other churches purchased land in the Xambre area, and gave encouragement and strength to our Xambre group. I continued the regular Bible studies with the church leaders of the area.

The Xambre church held several Spiritual Retreats on their grounds. Norm and Betty Charles gave tremendous assistance to the first Retreat. In addition to their spiritual ministry, they took care of the meal preparation. Accommodations for sleeping were a bit rustic—dried grass spread out over the floor and big canvases placed on top. Each person brought a sheet, blanket, and pillow. Adults lay scattered all over the canvas. The girls had one big classroom in the back of the church, and the boys slept in an empty house close to the church. At this first Retreat we had 40-50 people that slept-over every night of the Retreat.

God blessed in numerous ways as many made decisions for Christ, and close fellowship bonds developed within the families of these western churches.

In February 1967 we had another Spiritual Retreat in Xambre, extending the invitation to all of our Brazilian churches. We used the big Mission tent as a sleeping place for the boys. Again they gathered dry grass for bedding accommodations. It was "off season" for the drying of coffee and many big canvases were available. About 100 people stayed on the grounds.

Many other youth who did not regularly attend our church came from the city. Also many adults came for the evening services and sat in the back section. This filled the church to capacity each evening.

Following the service one evening we had an *After Glow* fellowship around a big bonfire built behind the church. This service was for *Youth Only* with inspirational singing and testimonies. Many of the youth had received numerous blessings during the meetings and wanted to share their experiences.

As the flames lowered, someone tossed two big sacks of sweet potatoes onto the hot coals. About a half hour later we had a great feast—delicious—some charred a little, but all were edible.

This service turned out to be the highlight of the Retreat—many "sleepers" did not settle down until well after midnight. We appreciated a place like the Xambre church for these Retreats. We all have wonderful memories of these special occasions.

Far too soon it became necessary to head back home. Even with very rustic sleeping quarters, God blessed us in many ways. Our youth lined the altar seeking a closer walk with God. Many had made first time decisions to follow Christ.

After these meetings the local people always helped clean up the church, and they did it with an excellent spirit. Before the meetings they prayed with anxious expectation of a good Retreat, and afterward they rejoiced in God's blessings during their time together, and our transformed Youth Group.

As a result of these meetings some of the youth made decisions to attend Bible School and became workers for Christ: others now have their own family and are faithfully active in their local churches: and many others moved up into the Rondonia area and are helping to establish churches on that new Frontier. As we visited them on our tours north, they often commented about the spiritual blessings they received at the Xambre Church Retreats.

The GreenAcre School in Maringa is our Mission boarding school. It began in February 1962 and, eventually, our children attended. Jackie taught our oldest son Rick at home for his first and second years. Then off to school he went for his third grade studies.

Little brother Ted began his first grade with his mother as teacher, and finished the year in Maringa. He had his 7th birthday far from home. Ted continued his entire schooling — except for our furlough years — at GreenAcre School, and graduated from 12th grade in 1973.

Separation from our children was never easy, but we often had business in Maringa and could visit them every few months. The boys were always anxious to get home for the holidays and their vacation periods. When the roads were good, it only took us about seven or eight hours to cover the 200 kilometers (125 miles). Then the time came when we preferred to travel at night with less traffic and dust. In case of rain, we also had fewer trucks to contend with.

One time when Rick was 11 and Ted, 9, we were traveling at night. Anita (5) and Michael (2) were sleeping in blankets in the back of the Jeep station wagon as usual. On a steep hillside the vehicle slipped over to the side of the road and into a small wash out. Both boys got out of the Jeep to help. Ted held the flashlight.

The clay soil was slippery — we could hardly stand up. With each step our shoes became heavier because the mud stuck to them. Then a light rain began to fall. It appeared to have set in for the rest of the night as it was so warm and humid.

Rick and I jacked up the car and put stones under the wheels. A shovel and big hoe went with us on most trips. After I had taken away the worst of the mud from in front of the wheels, Jackie "drove" while Rick and I pushed: Ted kept the light on the track.

It took more than an hour to get up the sharp incline and back on the road. Soaked to the skin and muddy, we climbed back into the Jeep. A short while later Rick said, "Isn't this wonderful!"

Not quite so enthused, I asked, "What is so wonderful?" He responded, "Just us all being together and working together!"

Rick had expressed how we all felt: *A Family United is a Great Joy.*

Michael, Anita, Ted, Rick, Jackie, and Dick

Chapter 13

Furlough—1967-1968

L eaving the Field for furlough in 1967 was much easier than in 1962. Now we had Bible School graduates over the churches: Mario, at Perola; Elcy, in Umuarama; and Sr. Ari, as lay pastor at Xambre.

While it is true that our support came from the Mission, we used our tithes and offerings to help needy families and to meet the local needs of the church. The churches of Perola and Umuarama had been constructed without any assistance from the Mission; the Perola church had been just freshly painted with paint purchased by the local church; no bills were outstanding against any of the churches; and a Subsidy Program for the pastors had been worked out between the Mission and the churches.

The Subsidy Program: Our Mission would help support the pastors for a period of five years. Each year a graduated reduced amount would be given to the pastor, and the church's portion increased accordingly; after five years, the church was expected to be self supporting.

As we left for our furlough home, we knew each pastor—and each church—needed much prayer to achieve this goal.

According to schedule, we returned to the U.S.A. in July 1967 for our 2nd furlough. We rented a furnished home located in the country, south of Elkhart, Indiana, near the Bethel Missionary Church. During that summer we attended the Prairie Street Camp Meeting near our home (Indiana), and the camps at Stayner (Ontario) and Ludlow Falls (Ohio).

In the fall, winter, and spring, I spoke at the Missionary Conventions of the United Missionary Church in Michigan, Ohio, Indiana, and (the state of) Washington.

Although I was never anxious to be out in deputation ministry, God blessed us and we saw that our people had a real concern for Foreign Missions. In speaking and meeting the people, we realized even more than before that our work progressed well in Brazil because of their many prayers.

When our year of furlough ended, we strongly felt that God wanted us to take a *Leave of Absence* from the Mission for one year to spend the time with our children.

God led us to purchase an old one-room red-brick schoolhouse—the Jonesville School—on the northwest corner of CR 7 and CR 30, in Harrison Twp, Elkhart County, Indiana. It became an entire family project to make this building into our home. During the summer months I worked at Holiday Rambler Recreational Vehicle factory. In the fall I received a one-year contract (1968-69) to teach the third grade at Jimtown Elementary public school close by (Baugo Community School Corporation). Jackie became the nurse at the Elkhart County Farm—a residential home for elderly and handicapped persons—east of our newly acquired home.

During the school year we all left home in the morning within a half hour. In the late afternoon we all returned within about an hour—coming from three different schools, and Jackie from about six miles in the opposite direction. Enthusiastically we worked together remodeling our home. It was an enormous project.

As missionaries, we had signed a pledge with our Mission that we wouldn't go in debt or leave any unpaid bills when we returned to our Field of service. We had been living within our budget, but had no credit rating. The old schoolhouse sat on a one-acre plot, but the banks would not loan the money. The owner then offered to sell the property to us on a Land Contract, if we paid $1,000 cash and the remaining $4,000 in payments. An uncle loaned us the down payment.

Our immediate goal was to fix it up, live there, and rent it out during our time in Brazil. The rent we would receive would be more than the remaining payments.

The family who had lived in it—about a year—had lowered the ceilings and made two bedrooms. The old school had two cloak-rooms: boys and girls—one on each side of the belfry-room entry. One cloakroom had been converted into a bathroom, and the other cloakroom became a storage room. An old coal/wood heater had been used for heat. However the heater had been removed before we purchased the building. Providing heat for the house became our first major task.

The basement was one big room. We decided to put in a forced air oil furnace, and completely remodel the basement with two bedrooms, a large family room with a fireplace, a laundry room, and a shower. With a full basement, we had a nice sized furnace room, too.

This meant a big double chimney needed to go up first, and the ductwork for the furnace must necessarily be in place before the installation of any ceiling tile. We enclosed the space under our entry way and former cloakrooms for the storage of potatoes, carrots, and other produce along with the jars of canned fruits and vegetables. Rick and Ted slept in the living room until their bedrooms—replacing the coal and wood bins—were ready.

We worked until midnight almost every night that year. God provided a warm late fall—the furnace went in just before Thanksgiving.

Although the winter presented a great challenge in many ways, I really enjoyed that year in the classroom. It wasn't easy with my teaching assignment, for I needed time for lesson preparation and grading papers. Rick and Ted helped grade a few papers. I believe that I learned as much that year as any student.

The year at home became one of the most practical years of our lives in drawing our family together. The big project of reforming the old school—an ideal project—brought us into a closer bond of fellowship and harmony. Our oldest son, Rick, expressed it this way, "We sure put a lot of love into this old school which is now our home!"

Project: "...Our Home."

As we began planning and preparing to return to Brazil, our family had a very difficult and extremely hard decision to make. Result: it seemed best to allow Rick to remain in the U.S.A. to complete his High School studies. Although anxious to return to Brazil, our sadness lay in leaving behind our oldest son Rick.

Chapter 14

Our Return to Brazil—1969

July 1969 found us again in Brazil—our 3rd term of service. We were assigned to start a new work in Umuarama. We had asked in 1965 to begin a work there. With a population of 25,000 to 30,000 people, Umuarama—now the crossroads of the western part of the state of Parana—would soon become the shopping and cultural center of the west.

I was permitted to continue teaching Bible in the extension program. But in order to have more time to concentrate in the new work, I had been asked not to assist the other churches which were now under the supervision of National pastors. However, several things had not worked out as planned with our pastoral set up.

During our ministry of overseeing the three churches, many local leaders had accepted responsibility for their church. But as the National pastors took over, the local leaders very gladly had given up their responsibilities. These young pastors were better prepared at leading singing as well as teaching classes. Our interior families, more conservative and influenced by the Pentecostal groups, left our churches family by family.

While the pastors preached tithing, each one seemed more convinced that if the local church didn't (or couldn't) raise the required support, the Mission would take care of the shortfall. Those who had been taught to support their pastor and to tithe were no longer in the churches.

With the constant movement of people in all of Brazil, the new settlers on the Frontier became even more unstable. From the very start more people were moving out of the church than new ones coming into the church. Also, the philosophy of allowing parents to take the responsibility of correcting their own children had greatly helped our ministry.

The frosts hit harder in Xambre causing more people to migrate from this area. Even with people leaving, Sr. Ari, the lay pastor, had the strongest work of the three churches. God had helped him in his leadership ability over the years. He received no financial support from the Mission, and the church members worked with him more like a team. As far as welcoming new people into the church and making them feel at home, Sr. Ari far surpassed even me with his ministry.

The Vila church in Umuarama had very few people still attending. When the young pastor took over the work, the members soon discontinued coming. Upon our arrival the National Church asked Sr. Valdemar, the lay pastor from Fazenda Peroba who recently moved to Umuarama, to take over the Vila church.

A nice home in Umuarama had been rented for us. But now its emptiness—Rick in the U.S.A. and three children (Ted, Anita, and Michael) at Boarding School in Maringa—left us feeling quite lonely with a certain type of sadness until the Holidays and semester breaks came. But once again we felt strength from the Lord to remain obedient and faithful to our calling. We cannot and do not count the cost when obeying God. He knows best the path that He has chosen for us.

In addition to renting a home for us, they also had purchased a large double lot in an area with no other church. We soon erected a big tent on the lot. Special services began nightly, and the meetings continued for more than a month. Some outstanding evangelists came to speak and help us. We also had the full cooperation of all our missionaries and National pastors.

God richly blessed these meetings. Big crowds came. People made decisions nightly. In a Catholic culture the people are familiar with Masses and Confessions, and at times a good proportion of the crowd came forward regularly for prayer. It was difficult to know how many first time genuine decisions were made: God knows these results better than man, anyway. But as time went by, we soon could tell which ones became faithful followers of the Way.

New converts need Bible study and spiritual nourishment. In some cases the new converts became immediate helpers in the services, and through home visitation we soon had entire families in attendance.

For the first time we had some new converts among the upper class of people. We had almost daily contact with the middle and upper class as we purchased gas and groceries, handled our financial matters at the banks, made various business deals in construction and other things, but there had been no contact with the these groups within the church. In fact, some of the pastors even thought that God had called them to work with only the poorer classes of people.

Sr. Osvaldo was one of the converts in the tent. He lived within a block of the tent site, and had come to most of the meetings from the very beginning. Several times I had talked to him, and prayed much for him. In his childhood he had attended an evangelical church. (I prefer to use the term *evangelical* because we have a positive evangelical message rather than protestant—*protestor*—against many things). I usually went over to the tent early to play Gospel music out over the PA system.

One night Sr. Osvaldo also came early and asked if he could give his testimony that night. He had accepted Christ as his Savior the previous evening. Although he hadn't come forward with the others when the altar call was given, he had accepted Christ right where he was seated. In his testimony he asked the Christians to pray for him, as he truly needed God's help in living for Him: Sr. Osvaldo was a cattle dealer.

Much different than in the U.S.A., most cattle farms are like ranches or large estates. A deal on cattle maybe anywhere from a few heads up to a couple thousand heads of cattle. Sometimes the cattle had to be moved several hundred miles. Most of the feeder cattle are driven along the back roads. On each deal the dealer also had the responsibility of moving the cattle. He had contacts with the cowboys who do the driving, and they usually scheduled the drives so they can camp each night, if possible, by a stream or river.

On these drives the cattle usually put on weight even though some may be on the road for as long as 30 days. A horse-drawn cart follows the herd to haul the newborn calves while enroute. Several old donkeys usually go ahead carrying a big pack of supplies. By using his Jeep, Sr. Osvaldo kept in contact with them daily to see that everything—supplies and all—was in order.

Much dishonesty hovered around most cattle deals. Sr. Osvaldo had connections and dealings with many men that had no church affiliations. While many Christians told him that he should get into some other business, I personally counseled him that "…we can be a Christian and a witness in most businesses … in his profession he can be truthful … and God will help him…"

Most of his dealings had been on Sundays and in bars. He changed this, and God blessed him. Although he will not go out on Sundays anymore, most of the buyers and sellers now respect his stand and make appointments to do business with him during the week.

At times he makes trips that take him away from town for a week or two, then usually on Sunday he visits a church in that area. When they eat a meal—even in bars—he asks permission from the others to say a prayer before the meals. When they drink alcoholic drinks, he accepts a soda or fruit juice.

Once in passing into another state, the Federal police at the check stop asked him if he carried any arms or weapons. He opened his briefcase and presented his Bible saying, "This is my sword."

When the police recognized that he was a Christian, they apologized for asking the question. Most of the other buyers and dealers had revolvers as they went into the Frontier country to buy cattle. However, on the Frontier almost everyone carries a knife or revolver for protection against snakes and wild animals.

One time I had the privilege of going along with him to observe the negotiation and purchasing process. On the ranches the herdsmen ride horses through the brush swamps bringing the cattle into big corrals. But almost all the owners live in the cities, so most of the deals are made in the town bar. After several days of talking, they go out to see the cattle, talk some more, and then close the deal.

Sr. Osvaldo is good natured in his spiritual life, and gives a personal testimony at every opportunity. He teaches the adult Sunday school class; has been the church treasurer; our deacon; and in the absence of the pastor, takes charge of the service.

Sr. Francisco Sales Ribeira, another one of the first men saved in the tent, had a large family. One by one, most of them accepted Christ as their Savior, and have been very active in the Youth Group and church services. He owned a small bazaar—a family project.

Sr. Francisco knew how to manage a business and meet people. He also taught his children to work. As they grew older, they worked in other stores and businesses in Umuarama. He kept his home open to the friends of his children. It became the natural meeting place of many of the town youth. Later, these contacts brought many other youth into the church. They were one of the first families to have a television in their home, and their home was almost always full of their children's friends, but they shut off the TV at church time, and invited everyone to go along to the services.

Sr. Francisco welcomed us at any hour of the day. At times he gave us much sound counsel in the administration of the church.

Sr. Altayr Machado and his wife Halina also made decisions in the tent. They owned a book store in Umuarama and sold Bibles and other religious supplies. At the time of their conversion they were continuing their studies at the University. Soon they had teaching positions in the Public School System and sold their book store. One of their greatest contributions to our Chapel in Umuarama was done through their finances. They had a good income; they tithed; and they had a great compassion for the needy and unsaved. Their children had stayed in our home many times while they attended classes. We enjoyed the grandparent-like role with their children.

Then, because of their education, Sr. Altayr and Sra. Halina received much better teaching positions in the southwestern part of Parana. When they moved in 1975, our Chapel family suffered a great loss. Before they left, we had a baptism service for new converts. We kept in contact: our relationship continued.

Many youth attended our tent meetings. Most of the special music and testimonies came from this group of young people. They began asking for more activities. We started having a volleyball game after the evening service. Very soon the youth became the biggest portion of our attendance. But a few of the mischievous boys in the area liked to slip around and turn out the lights in the tent.

It's the custom in Brazil for the light meter, or the fuse box with the big breaker switch, to be placed close to the inside edge of the property, or on the front outside wall of a home. This made an easy prank for a young person to go along and turn out the lights. We had someone keep an eye on this light switch—just another of the many jobs in caring for a tent service.

The tent continued to be used until a church could be built. From the start we received offerings toward this building project. I constructed a small model of the Perola church; put a hole in the top through which donations could be dropped; and a small locked door on the back to facilitate removal of the money. After this, we didn't take any more offerings for a building program. We announced nightly that they could "place their offerings in the church-box after the service."

As finances came in, we began to plan. An architect drew the design for us. We purchased the steel windows and wiring. When it became evident that we didn't have sufficient finance potential in our small group to build the big church, the plans had to be changed. The group decided that we should build the superstructure of the future parsonage and use it for the Chapel.

The parsonage in which we lived was very adequate, but belonged to the Lutheran mission. They didn't have a missionary in Umuarama at the time, and had rented the house to our Mission. We had offered to purchase it, but they didn't want to sell. More recently they had advised our Mission that they needed the house within six months time.

It worked out that I ordered materials and supervised the building of both the Chapel and the Mission house at the same time. However in the long run of things, our rent in Umuarama for the remaining portion of our term would have been more than the cost of construction. This is true in most parts of Brazil.

We lacked about $1,000 for the construction of the Chapel. Our investment in the windows had been almost the same amount that we needed. But these young Christians decided the windows had been a good investment toward the big church that we had planned. So we borrowed the $1,000 to immediately start the construction.

The groundbreaking ceremony was held in the back part of the tent which would become the back corner of the new Chapel. We hired a carpenter to work by the day, and volunteer workers came in to help.

By ordering the lumber, bricks, and other supplies for both buildings at one time, they only had to deliver them a few blocks apart. But I had to keep things straight on the ledger to know how much of each of the supplies went into the construction of each building.

In June of 1970 we dedicated the new Chapel—*Capela Evangelica* (Evangelical Chapel). The attendance dropped only slightly as we moved from the tent into the Chapel. These people became the faithful nucleus of our new work. We had good cooperation from these Christian workers, and a close fellowship developed among them—for this we thanked and praised God.

Each year we had about 40%-50% increase in inflation. Usually it took almost six months to a year from the time money is budgeted to buy or build, until the Mission Board in the U.S.A. approved and sent the finances. Since we didn't have sufficient funds to purchase a lot for the parsonage in the better part of town, we purchased a lot on the growing edge of town and built there.

Jackie always liked to design and plan homes. Now she had her opportunity. We brought a book of house plans with us from the States. In the book she found a floor plan that suited our needs better than any floor plan she had seen in town.

The exterior of the plan didn't differ much from some of the downtown area homes in Umuarama, or the larger cities of Brazil. It had plenty of closet space and could be built for less money than local comparable homes—a tri-level with four bedrooms on the upper level.

We used one of the upper rooms for my study. The lower level had a storage room, the garage, and a maid's room. (In our home we didn't use the term *maid* for our helper. We treated her as one of the family: she ate at our table.) The middle level consisted of our living room with a fireplace, a dining room, and the kitchen.

About three months after we moved in, we hooked up to electricity. The phone took longer—until the last week of this third term. Previously we made phone calls in town from the telephone company's Central Office.

During the construction of both buildings I did the work of a contractor, and at the same time helped a lot by using my power circular saw and drill. I don't believe a day went by that I didn't work on the job. Both buildings—Chapel and parsonage—were built for much less than any contractor would have charged, and we enjoyed the opportunity to work together with the people.

Pindorama soon needed a regular meeting place—a church. A group from Fazenda Peroba began holding regular services in this Frontier town. Temporarily they had rented a storage building from a grain buyer. Now the corn harvest loomed ahead, and the buyer needed his building.

Fazenda Peroba had fewer workers and many empty homes because of the hard frost. Much of the coffee land had been put into cereal grains: corn, soybeans, beans for eating, plus cotton. They had purchased a tractor and other equipment. The Mission group suggested that two houses be dismantled and the lumber used to build a nice smaller church. Another home could be dismantled for a parsonage, and also rebuilt in Pindorama. Shortly after making this decision, *they chose me* to supervise the project.

A lot of the farm workers from the (CSF) Peroba church volunteered their help. I moved to the farm to organize the dismantling and reconstruction, and returned to Umuarama only on the weekends.

Also at that time, I managed the farm. It felt good to be around the farm again and watch things progress. God gave me extra strength to carry the additional load. That summer Rick, our oldest son, came back from the States and worked along with me—what a great pleasure.

All five of our churches in the west—Perola, Fazenda Peroba, Xambre, Umuarama Chapel and Vila—accepted the invitation to the dedication of the Pindorama church in July 1971.

In that same month, July 1971, CSF sold Fazenda Peroba. About a year previous to the sale, I had been given the responsibility of managing the farm. With plans underway to sell the property, a front corner had been retained upon which to relocate the Peroba church and a home for the caretaker. Consequently, after the sale I had the responsibility of moving the big farm church and caretaker's home to its new location—a distance of almost a mile. God helped me as a contractor-builder.

Although I had some assistance from the Christians in the area, it took a lot of my time. Once again, for more than a month I returned to Umuarama only on the weekends.

In our 3rd term I enjoyed the responsibility for building/rebuilding three churches and three homes in addition to starting a new church work from scratch, and all the spiritual ministry of teaching and preaching.

For a part of this time I did not continue the formal Bible School Extension classes on a regular basis, but I did find time to be with some of these young pastors and lay pastors. Often they worked with me on the construction sites, and we had a lot of time for informal discussions. Sometimes this type of training is the most practical.

While working at the farm, I helped in the services as well as the services in the new work at Pindorama, and even dropped in on some of the services at Xambre. After having been away from Xambre for a few years, we renewed many old friendships.

Although the CSF farm had been sold, the coffee harvest was ours—and I had to be around the farm during the harvest. We sold the coffee in Umuarama, and I drove the farm truck: at that time I was the only person (on the farm) with a driver's license. I used the truck, planned my trips so I could be home more often, and arranged to take bricks back to the farm on my return trip. The bricks would be used in the foundation of the big church.

At Umuarama Jackie had all the responsibilities and duties that had been mine in addition to her regular schedule. She did a lot of visitation which is always necessary with a new church. These new Christians had a great concern for their friends and relatives.

But they needed counseling and guidance for themselves as well as to give counsel and guidance to their friends who were beginning their new Life in Christ. Help was needed desperately. But the Lord knows our need long before we do, and He knows the way to work out each circumstance just right.

A sincere Christian young man, who made a foolish mistake that caused him to lose out on his studies, needed a job—plus love and security—at the time of *our* need. He became the night guard and stayed in the tent. Later he—Paulo—became my main helper throughout the construction of the Umuarama Chapel and our home. After the tent came down, he lived in one room at the back of the Chapel. In addition to assisting with the carpentry work, he helped in the church services—leading the singing, taking charge of the Bible study when I couldn't be present, and other things.

On the farm Paulo became my right-hand-person—helping in the dividing of the coffee for the share-croppers, loading, and hauling the coffee to market. He put in some long hours that year with me. His ability as a carpenter and bricklayer really helped with each project on and off the farm.

Pindorama and the Peroba farm didn't have electricity. I borrowed a portable generator in order to use my electric drill and the circular saw. The native hardwood used in the framework of the buildings required the drilling of a small hole before driving a nail. By using the power saw I kept at least two carpenters busy nailing the boards in place. These projects took team effort and we praise God for the cooperation and loyalty of our Christians. We enjoyed great times of blessing in our fellowship as well as in the reality of the work accomplished.

Since most of the people had never seen a portable generator or circular skill saw, a large group always came to watch the action. Unbelievers came out of curiosity to see how the buildings were erected so quickly. Many times as I looked up, there were heads close to mine watching the electric saw at work.

One dear fellow—mentally challenged and laughingly called "the Mayor"—bumped into my helmet several times in getting close enough to watch the process. Everyone became aware of things happening on the tent site and they were ready to observe if Christians live as they preach.

Paulo continued to help me even after he married, and they lived in the little addition at the back of the Chapel. His faithfulness in every type of work became a blessing to everyone. Later they moved to Maringa, and the Lord provided another couple to be caretaker of the church and lot.

This newest couple among us had been Youth in our Fazenda Peroba church. Because they didn't have sufficient funds to exist on the farm, our Umuarama church group helped them financially. A few months after their move to Umuarama, their baby daughter became very ill with spinal meningitis. For several days the doctor didn't know if the babe would recover. Our Chapel group prayed, and God spared her life. God works in all ways and we give Him praise— even in sicknesses like this one.

Immediately this created a great spiritual awakening at the Chapel. Many came for prayer, and many others grew spiritually with increased trust in God. One of our converts began to pray for her unsaved neighbors: God answered her prayers.

Umuarama had not been an easy town to evangelize. Many people had migrated into this city during its relatively short time of exis- tence—15 years—and it now had a population of approximately 30,000 people.

The town had developed into a commercial center, and most of its people had an interest only in materialism, schooling, and sports. Many of the people living in the area of our church grounds were business men: store owners and Fazenda owners. As in most cities of Brazil, many poorer people of the working class lived in the same neighborhood as these businessmen. We had close contact with doctors, lawyers, and the upper class people as well as the lower economic groups of people.

Umuarama had about 20 evangelical churches, and a very strong Catholic Church Center with three outlying churches. Many of the evangelical churches had been founded by their members who had moved on west with the Frontier. So most of their churches were not strong, nor were they winning many new converts.

The Pentecostal churches had their Central Church (mother church) located in Umuarama. They were growing fast with many branch churches throughout the area. In addition to winning souls, they also proselyted from the other churches. Very few of their pastors worked only in Umuarama: some had as many as six or more preaching points throughout the area. But statistics do not completely tell the truth.

As a new pioneer country, northern and western Parana had wide open opportunities to evangelize. When people moved into an area like this, they have almost complete freedom—meaning there is much less group pressure from family and the Catholic Church to hinder true Bible based evangelization: whereas in the more stable and older cities in Brazil, there is still persecution against evangelical groups.

Because of this spiritually fertile field, many evangelical churches and missions moved into the Parana area. Some statistics would indicate that nearly half of the population in our area is now Christian. Of these, some people have been baptized three, four, or five times among the different churches. The area is not as Catholic as their church states, nor is there as strong of an evangelical body of believers as the Protestant churches claim.

Umuarama had more than 20 Spiritist centers when we moved there. These groups influenced many people with their satanic power—so strong that we ran into demon possession right in our own church services. From experience I can say, they had an influence in all of the churches. In addition to this, most unchurched people lived in constant danger of the influence of Spiritism without the protection of the blood of Christ that the believers had.

Spiritist healers, surgeons, and leaders of these groups actually used Bible scriptures in their teachings. Many of them hand out literature and publicly announce when one of their medium leaders or healers would be coming to their Center. Many people became involved unaware that it was satanic. The origin of these groups began in the days of slavery: as the African slaves came to Brazil, they brought their religions with them.

One particular Sunday afternoon I visited the home of one of our Christian families whose neighbor's house stood less then 30 feet away—separated only by a wooden picket fence to give their yards some privacy. Both homes were simple wooden structures, and voices in conversation could be heard easily from either house.

The neighbor had called in a medium to heal his sick daughter. The medium and his group brought with them a drum or two to drive the evil affliction out of the girl. I heard right here in Umuarama, Parana, Brazil, the same things I had heard my uncles—pioneer missionaries—describe of the witch doctors in Nigeria, West Africa. The noise from the drums along with weird yelling and howling from the house next door became so great that we couldn't visit inside the home of our friends.

Finally we joined hands and prayed the protective power of Christ and His blood over their home and family. It felt oppressive to be near this activity. As we left, I suggested that it might be better for them to visit their friends and get away from this satanic power.

Our tent campaign in Umuarama began with a very good Brazilian evangelist. He had experience in casting out demons, and had been invited to pray in several homes for family members or friends who were demon possessed. I will never forget one of these experiences.

Our evangelist had been asked to come to the home of a young lady possessed with a demon. He asked all who were not Christians to leave as the freed demon might possibly enter into them: demons go from one body to another body—preferably a human body.

First, we joined hands and prayed for the protection of the blood of Christ over us. Then we laid hands on the girl and began praying for her. As we did this, the dogs in the neighborhood began to bark. Even the old mule—tied with a rope—began to jump around. The girl gasped for breath, and coughed. Finally she had a Peace on her face that her parents had not seen in years.

Through this experience we realized that we needed more power from God. God had blessed us and helped us many times, but we needed something more. The Spiritist mediums and healers seemed to have more courage than we had in our churches. Also we needed much more discernment in situations and power to cast out demons. We observed that the Pentecostals and spirit-filled leaders had power to deal very effectively with the demon possessed person.

Special evangelical meetings had been announced in the local high school sponsored by the Revived Presbyterian churches. We always had a close friendship with each of the pastors in our area.

One Saturday evening our service dismissed early, and we slipped into the back of the church to visit their meeting. Many sought Christ as their Savior; others went forward to be healed; and some went into private rooms to have demons cast out.

In the meeting they announced that "...several visiting pastors didn't have a place to stay for the night...." Since we had plenty of room, about six of their pastors came to our home overnight. After having coffee together, we retired. Later I learned that several of these pastors had stayed up for several hours longer praying for us.

Sunday morning we visited their first service as our service came later in the day. God began showing us our need for more of His power. That afternoon one of their leaders, Pastor Jonathan who became a very dear friend of ours, met with us in a classroom and led us into the experience of the Baptism of the Holy Spirit. We did not speak in tongues at that time. Later, in private prayer at home, the Lord gave us that gift also. The experience greatly changed our ministry.

My ministry had been more in the teaching of God's Word. Since the baptism of the Holy Spirit, God gives me His message as I meditate and pray before the service. My time in sermon preparation has been greatly shortened. Now I have more time for my devotional life and study. It's now much more of a pleasure to be a minister: sermon preparation and Bible studies are no longer a burden, but a joy.

Jackie shared in this experience with a greater compassion for the needy; and for both of us came the gift of discernment. This gift is invaluable in knowing if a person is drunk, drugged, demon possessed, or oppressed. At times, it can be any combination of these. We need only to depend wholly upon God to help us in this type of ministry. Our complete dependence upon God in times such as this is almost too sacred to talk about—*nothing in us, but only the power of God working through us.*

A call for prayer at the altar is given at nearly every service. With the Catholic influence, the Brazilians were uninhibited to gather regularly around the altar for prayer. God is ready to help and strengthen each one of us in proportion to our humility, faith, and trust in Him. Many came to pray for their unsaved relatives and friends: others came because of sickness and physical afflictions: still others came for salvation for themselves.

My gift has not been in any one ministry. God has used me in healing and the casting out of demons as well as in pastoral and Bible teaching ministries. Several times as I prayed for an individual I felt power pass through me to the individual—a little like touching an electric fence. The more we saw the power of God at work, the more we wanted to give all the praise and honor to Him. If anything is accomplished, it is nothing of us, but God working through us.

Not only did our ministry change, but our whole outlook and attitude changed. I had been too much program- and time-centered on what I wanted to do. Since the experience (of the Holy Spirit), I have wanted to be more Spirit controlled, and have the freedom so Christ could work through me even more than previously.

In preparing for a church service, I continued with a brief program or outline in my Bible. But many times I looked at the program only to make sure of the name of a special speaker, singer, or musical group. In addition to the guitars and Jackie's accordion, the people clapped in rhythm to the singing as they enthusiastically expressed their love for God. With the more devotional songs—just before prayer—there was no clapping of hands, only a beautiful quiet reverence.

Most of the people brought their Bibles and searched for the passages referred to in the message. As long as I heard pages turning I continued to explain the background of the passage, its purpose, and maybe the history of the author, until everyone found the passage. Often the older Christians gave the newer Christians help in finding the chapter and verse. Most of the youth in Umuarama attended school, could read very well, and were glad to be involved in the reading of the Word—even coming to the front of the church to read the scripture.

After-church-fellowship seemed more like a family reunion. If they didn't have time to give their testimony or tell of God's blessings on their life during the service, they told it to each other after the service: *no one hurried home after any service.*

On one occasion I arrived at the church about fifteen minutes before the service. A friend who lived nearby invited me to the birthday party of his one-year-old son, saying many of his friends and neighbors would be there. It's a Brazilian custom to have big birthday parties. Most Christians invite their pastor to have a religious service before the refreshments and games.

I replied that I couldn't come because of the service starting soon. But he had already announced that I would be the speaker at the party. So I reconsidered, and asked if we could come just a little late: "We would begin our evening service at the church and then bring our entire group over to help in their meeting."

He agreed, saying there would be "...plenty of refreshments ..."

We began the service; rehearsed the choruses and hymns to be sung at the gathering; and one of our deacons stayed at the church to bring any late comers that might show up. God really blessed this birthday party.

When we arrived, the living room and front yard were filled with people and the tables were loaded with refreshments. They made room for our group, and the singing was excellent with unfamiliar voices joining in. Many of the people present would never have come to church. Had we stuck to our regular programmed meeting, we would have missed one of our best meetings of the year with nearly 100 in attendance.

A few years later this same man became stuck in the mud. He slid completely off the road with his VW bug. We saw his situation on our way to a service in Perola, and got out of our vehicle and into the mud and rain, to push him back on the road. Although he isn't a Christian as yet, we want to continually show Christian love toward him, and others, in everything.

Chapter 15

Trips to the Frontiers

To Rondonia: In their interest and compassion for each one of our families, Norm and Betty Charles traveled many miles to keep in contact and encourage those who had left the Fazenda Peroba coffee farm. Sometimes Norm drove the tractor all night to have more time for these trips and visits away from the farm. Many of these families had moved to the new territory in Rondonia.

With good connections and road conditions, a person could travel the 1500-2000 miles to Rondonia in three days. About half of the roads would be dirt roads that could be sandy or muddy with gravel or stones only on the steep hillsides. The other half—asphalt—would have big pot holes that at times can be worse than the dirt roads.

In July 1970 Norm and Betty Charles invited us to go with them. About 18 months earlier they had made a fast trip up to Rondonia, driving day and night by rotating drivers. Because of the busyness on the farm and one of their sons leaving for college, they felt they couldn't be away for any length of time, and had decided to drive straight through.

On the way home Norm fell asleep at the wheel and rolled the VW bus. Betty had an injured back. But they rolled the vehicle back on its wheels; placed blankets over the suitcases to make a bed for Betty; and God miraculously brought them home.

We accepted Norm's invitation as we also felt the need to make this evangelistic trip to this northern Frontier. We made plans to drive only in the daylight hours in order to "see the country" and not take any chances of someone falling asleep. However, we had plenty of drivers as eight of us crowded into the bus for this long trip—Norm and Betty; their son-in-law, Cleber; their helper-maid, Iracema, and her boyfriend; another missionary, Merv Traub; Jackie and I.

The luggage rack on top of the mini-bus held all our baggage. It took the weight of eight passengers inside the light bus to counter-balance the weight on the roof. The driver needed to get used to steering the vehicle because of the over-the-limit weight.

Secretly I questioned the advisability of taking the young couple—Iracema and her boyfriend: the only ones who couldn't speak English. Without them, we had a load. However, it was Norm's vehicle—we had been invited to go along—it was his decision which ones among us should go on the trip. It turned out that this young couple was about the biggest blessing of the trip.

Iracema knew by memory more than 100 choruses, hymns, and scriptures put to music. We used hymn books for the ones she didn't know by memory, and filled the many long hours of traveling with singing and scripture.

We took along Bibles, pieces of literature, and thousands of tracts. At every stop for gasoline, food, or lodging, we distributed the tracts along with personal witnessing. On one occasion Betty went into the kitchen to witness to the cooks: some accepted Christ as their Savior. Several times along the way we held religious services.

We stopped for the night at a rustic hotel in the pioneer city of Vilhena, located on the border of the territory of Rondonia, Mato Grosso. The front room of the hotel doubled as the bus stop and terminal. The hotel announced an evening service over their PA system. As evening approached, many people gathered around for an open air service.

While Jackie played her accordion more people came until there were more than 100 people standing around. Each of us gave a short testimony and meditation. Then Cleber, the Brazilian Bible School graduate among us, brought an evangelical message. Six people stepped forward to make a decision; others came with special needs, or for an illness.

The hotels and dormitories for sleeping caused us to realize more than ever that we were on the Frontier. The beds had only straw or grass mattresses, and the electricity was generated by a one-cylinder diesel motor.

This small power plant served the hotel, restaurant, gas pumps, and the motor on the well. This diesel motor ran from dark until about 10:30 p.m. The rooms used candles.

During the day they used hand pumps to fill the gas and diesel tanks of vehicles; and each evening, a large water tank. Because many trucks, buses, and other vehicles stopped during the day, most of the water tanks became empty by mid-day or shortly thereafter. But the people continued to use the bathrooms without water to flush the stools.

As the others unloaded our mini-bus, I usually went into the restrooms and began flushing toilets to get them cleaned up so we all could take showers after being on the hot dusty roads all day. Some places even had the luxury of electrical showerheads—hot water. Otherwise we refreshed ourselves in cold water to wash off dust and sweat.

Some of the hotel dormitories were set up for the men to sleep in one section, and the ladies in another. Iracema didn't want to sleep alone, so usually the ladies slept in the large bedroom with her. After the generator stopped we used candles and carried flashlights. Several times we ate an early breakfast by candlelight.

A major problem in the northern territories is distribution of gasoline and diesel fuel. It is all trucked in from deposits along the Amazon River, and often the roads are impassable or the supply trucks break down without a garage nearby. This leaves many stations without petroleum. With at least 30 miles between stations, we would never pass a gas station without filling the tank. One station—a very new one—filled an old five-gallon kerosene can, carried it to our vehicle, and siphoned it into the tank.

Many of the trucks and buses carry extra tanks, or cans, of fuel to make it to the next station on the long trip between Porto Velho and Curitiba. Some of the trucks may sell fuel to a vehicle stalled along the road, but others will say they have "just enough" for their own trip.

At our destination we enjoyed an unbelievable reception. They hugged and kissed us, and were starved for news of their friends, relatives, and the churches. Norm had his cassette recorder with him and played tapes of personal greetings from both relatives and church members. They listened intently, and actually cried when they heard the sound of familiar voices.

Word of our arrival soon spread. Immediately they began scheduling services for every night—mostly home services to invite all their neighbors. Every day we visited in their homes. Several times we made the 15 kilometer (9.5 mile) trip into Vila Rondonia for supplies. One evening we held an open air street service in this Frontier town.

The insects were terrible. Usually a swarm of blood-sucking gnats surrounded us all day long: at night, mosquitoes and vampire bats. The insect repellant kept the gnats away, and smoke from the smudge fires protected us from the mosquitoes. But a small girl from one of our families had a puncture on her big toe where a vampire had sucked blood the previous night. Later the family learned that if they hung a stalk of green bananas in their home, the vampires will eat the bananas rather than suck blood.

Their shelters have roofs that shed water, and walls made of split palm trees. As the palm trees dry, cracks are left between the wooden slats—wide enough to stick your hand through. However, in the hot and humid climate, the cracks permit air to circulate. The families plan to build better homes in the future as they can afford them.

The living room is the largest room of their home: usually half of the structure is living-dining room and kitchen. The remainder is divided into bedrooms, and storage space for food supplies including their harvest. Friends and relatives who often sleep overnight will lie on sacks of beans, rice, corn, or cotton—coffee and cocoa beans will be added at a future date. When they build a better home, this shelter will be used entirely for storage.

They had constructed a small church for worship. From the outside it looked just like one of their homes. But inside, there were no partitions or crude mud cook stove as in their homes. The palm leaves served very well to shed the rain. Our group slept and stayed in this simple church building. Although it rained hard several times, the roof didn't leak. It appears they copied their style of building from the Indians.

We strung up a few blankets for curtains to make two rooms — the ladies slept on one side, and the men slept on the other side. We covered the dirt floor with a canvas, and laid our sleeping bags and blankets on top of it. A couple hammocks were hung above the sleepers on the floor. During the night we heard mice, insects, and the big bugs that lived in the nests built in the leaf-thatched roof.

Betty and Norm taught us much in the realm of faith in Christ, and genuine faith in prayer. When Iracema became carsick within a few hours of leaving Maringa, we had to stop along the road. Norm and Betty led us in a special time of prayer for her: she wasn't sick again during the entire trip.

The lens on my camera stuck as many cameras do in this climate of high humidity and heat. We approached the area where I wanted to take lots of pictures of the Frontier and its people, and we were thousands of miles from any camera shop. Betty simply prayed for the camera: it worked for the rest of the trip. A year or so later the lens stuck again. A technician in Curitiba advised that in the tropics, camera lenses need another kind of lubrication. He cleaned it, and used some type of graphite against friction.

Our visit in the north was all too short. But each of us had obligations and other responsibilities awaiting our return, and knew we couldn't be away longer than these three weeks. Each day had been full of activities in visiting, along with preaching and teaching the many people who so willingly listened. In addition to our visits and prayers during the day, we held nightly services.

We brought many supplies with us for the people: Bibles, tracts, and literature; a large bottle of bottled gas and a gas light; a record player and records; and left many items of our personal clothing with them. I thought we would be lighter during the trip home. Instead, the load had become heavier as we began loading items the people brought us—Brazil nuts, bananas, and other gifts. We found we had much more weight than when we arrived.

As we finished loading the vehicle for our return trip, it began to rain and my rheumatism became worse. After sleeping on the damp ground a few nights during our stay, I slept in a hammock just to make my joints bearable and to be able to get along. Our clothes had been wet from perspiration most of the time, and would dry on our bodies as we went visiting from house-to-house: the worst situations for rheumatism.

The time came to say farewell to everyone who came to see us off. In addition to the messages taped on Norm's cassette recorder, we accepted many letters to take back to friends and relatives in *the South*. Some families brought more of the green banana stalks which had to be tied on top. Many tears were shed in the final hugs and farewells. We gathered around for one last prayer together, and off we went in the cloud of dust.

It seemed that we left part of our hearts with the people in Rondonia. Life is so hard for these people on the Frontier, and the opportunities for Christ are so great. We pray for them daily, and in almost every church service.

The crowded conditions of the VW bus didn't give me room to stretch out my legs, and the condensation began dripping from the roof of the van. Soon after getting on the road, we stopped at a small settlement to buy bread, fruit, and some things for our lunch. The pain of my rheumatism bothered me so much I could hardly bear it.

While Norm went to purchase the food items, Betty prayed for me. Immediately the pain began to leave my legs and body, and within a half-hour I had *absolutely no pain*—the rain still came down, and the moisture still dripped from the roof. I surely did praise God for Betty's prayer of faith, and for His healing power.

Their prayer ministry among the Brazilians was just as great. With no doctors in the area to help, and the hospitals so very inadequate, many needed prayer. Among Christians it is only normal to go to God first. He is ready to help us if we have faith in Him.

With each mile we drove, we knew we carried a load much too heavy for our vehicle. We stopped at a new sawmill to fill our fuel tank—no fresh fruit here. Several families had just arrived from the south. Gladly we gave them most of the heavy banana stalks. This also created another opportunity to give our testimonies along with some tracts.

The trip home was a long one, but we had good fellowship among ourselves as we got to know and appreciate one another better. A tire or two gave out on the trip; the vehicle needed a complete tune-up; all springs, bolts, doors, and the motor had to be checked over, tightened, and aligned. A 5000 mile trip on Frontier roads will give a beating to any vehicle.

To Belem (1971): The city of Belem—near the mouth of the Amazon River—was the center of commerce and business organizations in the north, in the same way Sao Paulo related to southern Brazil. Because so many of our people had headed north, we wanted to get as much information as possible concerning the area, and regarding the Homestead movement.

We found the Government was opening up 13 areas in the Amazon Basin for these Brazilian pioneers: the territory of Rondonia was only one of the areas in the southern part of the Basin. So far, the people from our area had only moved to Altamira and Rondonia, and our church members from Parana had only moved to Rondonia.

A friend of ours was considering opening a Bible School in Altamira and wanted information. So for us the trip had two purposes: we sought more knowledge of this *free land in the north*; and we wanted *a nice trip with our family* as Rick would be coming from the U.S.A. to join us for this trip.

During our third term Rick, our oldest son (16), stayed in the U.S.A. to continue his high school studies (junior and senior years), and begin Bible School training. He lived with relatives and friends in Ohio. Now with high school finished, he came to visit us in Brazil before entering Bible School. We planned this trip—a getaway from our heavy schedule—so we could all be together again as much as possible after being separated approximately two years: 1969-1971.

We planned to meet Rick at the Congonhas airport in Sao Paulo. We had a Mission meeting in Maringa the previous day, and drove our VW van—*Kombi*—all night to arrive in time to meet his flight. We had made good time and stopped along the road outside the city to rest for an hour or so. A fog set in.

When we awakened we could see—very hazily—only about 50 feet in front of the vehicle. This made our trip into the city a very slow one. The Lord helped us to catch the signs, and we drove right to the airport just in time for the scheduled arrival of Rick's flight.

Inside the airport an attendant informed us that the flight had been held up in Rio de Janeiro until the fog cleared here in Sao Paulo. But actually the plane had been circling the city for hours awaiting the "cleared to land" message from the radio tower.

Time passed.

They began making plans to land the plane at the airport in Campinas, and send the passengers back to Sao Paulo by bus. Instead, the fog lifted and the plane landed safely. Happy and excited, we headed back to Parana.

Rick arrived at the time Fazenda Peroba had been sold and I had charge of moving the Peroba church and home for the caretaker. So for about a week or 10 days Rick helped finish the moving and reconstruction of the two buildings. The Brazilian farm manager, Sr. Mariano, looked after the farm in my absence, and my beloved helper, Paulo, took over the supervision of the church services until our return.

The trip to Belem became a camping trip. We could not afford to stay at a hotel every night, and we wanted to "just be together". Each night we tied one side of a canvas to one side of the VW van, and staked down the other side. We removed the middle seat from the van and set it out under the canvas beside our two folding cots.

Our three sons slept outside on the seat and two cots; Anita, our daughter, slept inside on the front seat of the van; Jackie and I slept on blankets on the floor of the van. By morning the floor did get a little hard, but I had room to stretch out.

We had our small watch dog along—an excellent guard. No one could have come close without awakening us. He would have attacked them.

Every morning at daybreak we had breakfast and went for a swim before breaking camp. Usually we ate lunch on the run—fresh fruit, such as bananas or oranges along with baloney and cheese sandwiches. About 6:00 p.m. we stopped at a restaurant for a hot meal. These restaurants served family style meals with all the beans and rice a person could eat along with plenty of meat: four dinners for the six of us left scraps for our dog. We fed him once a day plus water. He was a good traveler with no road sickness. After our evening meal we drove several more hours before making camp again by some small stream or river to wash off the dust and take a swim.

The old road bed made a nice place to set up camp. The first bridges that had been built just cleared the water. When the improved roadway came in, they built the new bridges high above the ravine so the traffic didn't need to go down into the valley and climb the steep grade on the other side.

By picking a spot like this, we could camp under the bridge, wash off the dust from our journey as we cooled off from the heat, have our devotions, and relax while visiting with our children as a family.

God protected us and gave us an excellent place to camp each night. If we didn't fall asleep right away, we sang choruses. We could feel God's protection over and around us. Several times the big vampire bats flew into our van at night, but didn't attack anyone. Anita became afraid when it bumped or fluttered around the top of the van, but they soon left. Camping kept the cost of our trip low— we couldn't have afforded this trip any other way.

Most of the distance we had dirt roads. Without a side wind, the dust became bad at times. On one occasion we had to pass a truck that just crawled up the steep grade at about 10 mph. It left a trail of dust about a half mile long. What a relief to get ahead of a truck like that one. Between Brazilia and Belem all the roads were of dirt, and rough like a washboard.

Some of this area hadn't had much rain, and the people suffered from the drought. We encountered many people carrying water a long distance for their household use. A few people used donkeys to carry two kerosene cans filled with water on each side of the animal. Others carried containers of water on their head. As we learned how they had to live, we better understood their problems.

Belem—in the most northern area and on the Atlantic Ocean—is the commercial capital of the north. Most of their trade is carried by riverboats. Only a few of the larger boats had refrigeration. The beef and fish is dried and salted down in much the same way as it was done in the early days of western Parana.

This dried meat does not look appetizing—in fact, it smells a little rotten or putrid. We've been served this meat in restaurants and in homes of the nationals. It really doesn't taste too bad. However, I have never bought any of it for our family to use. But this dried, salty meat stood piled high in big stacks all along the wharf and in the warehouses.

A few more modern passenger liners had regular schedules going up the Amazon River at least as far as Manaus, and even farther during high tide: ocean freighters also are able to travel beyond Manaus at high tide.

Most of the old riverboats are about 50-60 feet in length, and approximately 12 feet wide. They have upper and lower decks, and are driven by a big diesel motor. The passengers bring their own hammocks which are tied to opposite sides of the boat. Their pigs, chickens, and baggage rest on the floor underneath. Usually no meals are served. Each person must take along their own lunch and serve him or herself.

The hammocks appeared to be two or three deep—one above the other. Of course, the pigs and chickens had their legs tied together so they could not get away, and would stay where they were placed. I've been told many people prefer to sleep on top of the roof—the upper deck—at night. But in case of rain, the top deck becomes the roof.

As we watched these boats pull away from the dock, it seemed unbelievable how many people and animals had crowded onto each riverboat.

With many streams and rivers entering the Amazon, some of the boats are chartered for specific runs, and others make regular runs between homes or villages that have no other means of communication except by the riverboats. Because this is the least expensive way to travel, many of the Frontier people use these boats to get to their future homes in these Amazon jungle areas. Most riverboats take two or more weeks to make their round trip. We had considered going to Altamira on one of the boats but couldn't make good connections and actually, we didn't have the time to make an extra side trip.

Our visit to the wharfs with all of the odors and lack of refrigeration must have been very much like the time of Columbus—these docks seemed like an entirely different world in our day and age.

These rivers have been the principle mode of transportation throughout the Amazon Valley. With the homestead movement, the people are heading out by all ways and means to get there. The trans-Amazon Highway was beginning to open up the north for buses, trucks and other motored vehicles. As we passed the eastern end of this big highway, we could see that the first one hundred miles or more was already passable: it connected with the Belem-Brazilia highway on which we traveled.

We enjoyed our visit and stay in Belem, and received the information we wanted. We stayed with the Wycliffe Bible Translators who had nice headquarters in Belem, and a rest camp on the outskirts of the city. Wycliffe worked among the Indians using small planes and radios to keep in contact with each of their workers.

We wanted to visit with them and learn more of their work. They permitted us to stay in one of their homes about four or five days while we were in the area. We visited with them nearly every evening, and our children enjoyed playing with their children. Their missionary school—equipped with a basket-ball court, soccer court, table tennis, and more—was located here at the Center.

The translators go out and live with the Indians in the Amazon area to learn their language—not to bring them to civilization, but to give them the Love of God where they live. By no means is this an easy job. As the Center makes their daily radio contact with each worker, they also deliver supplies to the various camps as needed. After several months the workers come back to the rest camp for a period of relaxation, rest, and renewal.

Their dairy project and excellent Brown Swiss cattle attracted my attention. The project supplied the group with plenty of milk and dairy products. Many of the calves were taken in to the different Indian tribes, and villages.

What a real blessing for us to *relax, rest, and renew* at this Center. Now the time had come for us to head back home.

After a day of travel we again encountered the eastern end of the trans-Amazon Highway. A large sign pointed west toward Altamira. This old port city on the Amazon became famous during the time Brazil was being recognized as the great rubber producing center of the world. But the road to Altamira was not open: we were unable to visit the city's fast growing Homestead Center.

While in Belem some agronomists told us that the climate and soil conditions in Altamira were very similar to Rondonia. Later a friend brought me a soil sample. When analyzed, the sample verified this to be true. Also equivalent was its production of Brazil nuts, rubber, and cocoa beans.

During our last night on the old dirt road, it rained hard—all night. We slept in a hotel. We were very glad to get back on the asphalt again and soon arrived home. Our trip back home had been just as enjoyable and eventful as the trip north.

Many people—Christians and non-Christians—came to us for information regarding the Northern area. In addition to this, we had all of our pictures to show them. Our goals had been met: we learned a lot, and had the necessary information for the people; and our family had a joyful time together. But now our vacation had ended, and Rick had a plane to catch.

It was hard to part with our oldest son—to watch him fly off alone to begin his Bible School training in the States. At least all of us had our hearts full of the memories of that trip—more than a vacation—it was a wonderful time of *just being together*.

Immediately I had to be at the Peroba farm. Most of the coffee had been contracted on shares, and the contracts with the workers expired with the harvest. I needed to be around for the completion of the harvest and sale of the crops. Because I was on the farm much of the time and knew many of the workers who needed work, it had been easy for me to schedule and oversee the dismantling, relocation, and rebuilding of the remaining two buildings.

It was hard to see our Christian families move away, yet we helped many of them as they settled elsewhere. Those who really wanted to stay were given work by the new owner. However, we had given extra privileges to the workers on this Christian farm which would not be continued by the new owner: not many families were interested in staying.

Chapter 16

Last Year of our Third Term

In January of 1971 the National Church appointed me the supervisor over the six western churches: Xambre, Perola, Pindorama, Fazenda Peroba, and the two churches in Umuarama. Within approximately three years, the Chapel at Umuarama had become the biggest church in the area: the dedicated Christians and some good business men made it financially sound and generous. In fact, the Chapel helped support the fund for National pastors in other churches being served by a pastor or a lay pastor.

I accepted the assignment with the condition that I could contact Bethany Bible School (Altonia, Parana) for more assistance. They had several young men who were seeking opportunities to get some practical experience in the ministry.

The first Bible School graduate from Maringa that came as pastor to the Vila church didn't get off to a good start. He took charge of directing all the services—the singing, the preaching, and the visitation. The people let him do everything. Soon, because of a clash in personalities, the large family that had founded the church just went to another church. This meant that Sr. Valdemar had a heavy struggle to keep things going. His health was failing, and the work had not gone ahead as it should. Sr. Valdemar handed in his resignation as lay pastor of the Vila church in Umuarama. Then God stepped in.

Our Chapel youth went with us to the Vila services. A young Bible School student from Bethany—Gustavo—came every weekend. The attendance came right back almost immediately. Many pre-teenagers lived around the church. This created a good Sunday school. In addition to the classrooms in the building, we had two classes meeting on the lawn under the shade trees. Once again people filled the small church for any special service.

Cidinha, a Bible School graduate from Maringa, also came out to assist. She taught in the public school system, and her financial support helped the Chapel. With no other home available, she stayed with us as one of the family. Our love and appreciation for her grew: both the Chapel and Vila churches loved and respected her ministry.

But Sr. Valdemar, who could no longer lead the church, did not want to leave. He continued to be a great asset to the church body as Gustavo and Cidinha gave new life and enthusiasm to the group.

Many of the people from the other four churches had migrated from the area. Slowly more were leaving than new ones coming in. We tried to encourage the pastors and lay workers, and worked with them as best we could. However, my time was limited due to the emphasis placed on our regularly scheduled Theological Education by Extension (T.E.E.) classes. No longer could I assume the responsibilities of the local leadership in the churches. Our goal was to encourage them, and help them to have a vision of the potential they had in Jesus Christ to carry on His work of evangelism. The members who moved on also needed much prayer to continue to be a witness wherever they went. Most of them kept in contact with us and other church leaders.

Sr. Jose Rodrigues who had been one of my main students in the T.E.E. classes, moved into the rebuilt parsonage in Pindorama. He would be pastoring the church there, and also the Fazenda Peroba church. God had saved him from Spiritism and given him good discernment regarding satanic power. We kept close brotherly contact with each other.

Sr. Jose had nine children which made it impossible for him to attend our Bible School in Maringa. He had mature judgment in making decisions, and I tried to do everything that I could to help him as he pastored these two churches. Some of the Christians who left the CSF farm (Fazenda Peroba) left their tithe money from their coffee harvest with the local church. With this money we purchased a horse and cart to help transport Sr. Jose and his family between the two churches.

God had blessed the Chapel in Umuarama, and the leaders developed quickly. Sr. Osvaldo, the converted cattle dealer, matured fast in his spiritual life. He had church training in his youth, and the people of the entire area greatly respected his experience as a business man. Enthusiasm grew, and the people brought in more of their families and neighbors. We had a very active youth group who willingly helped in the services of other churches as well as in all of the services of the local church. Most Sunday evenings the Chapel was filled to capacity.

For many years the special Christmas program—a drama—had been the highlight of the year. Then it seemed everyone wanted to be a spectator, and not a participant. Gradually the program became smaller and just for the children. But this year—1971—the youth had a desire to have a more meaningful program and promised to do their best by fully participating.

A young mechanic and his wife—recently converted—said they would like to help. The group asked Jackie to coach them, and rehearsed many hours. They prayed that the program would not be just for entertainment this Christmas, but for souls to be converted. They spent the remaining weeks busily preparing for this special Christmas Program.

Finally the day arrived. Many personal invitations had been distributed—the Chapel was packed, and many unsaved relatives and friends were present. The presentation went well. At the climax, I gave an altar call for people to come forward for prayer. Seven people responded, and the Christians gathered around them to pray. What rejoicing and praising God. It was one of the greatest services we ever had. The group presented the same program again in four other churches.

The Vila church in Umuarama also took on more enthusiasm and growth in 1971. A church of another denomination in Londrina came in and held a big tent campaign. Their tent blew down, and the Vila church helped them in their emergency. Also many of our members cooperated in assisting with the remaining services of the campaign. Because this denomination didn't have a work of their own in the area, some of their converts came to the Vila church. With the help of Cidinha, Gustavo, and the group from the Chapel, we gave excellent assistance to the pastoring in this new area.

Sundays always held a full schedule. The Sunday school at the Chapel began at 9:30 a.m. and we couldn't get away from there until almost 12:00 noon. We rushed to have our noon meal and be at the Vila for their 1:00 p.m. Sunday school. Then I put one of the Bethany students in charge of the evening service at the Vila, and returned back to the Chapel for their evening service. This made a busy Sunday.

The midweek Bible study and prayer meeting met on Tuesday night at the Vila and on Wednesday night at the Chapel. On Saturday evening our youth usually invited the youth from the Vila to come to the Chapel for a Youth Night Service.

The Xambre church—our first church in Brazil—has been the center of our work in the west since 1955. Many of our Christians first came into contact with the Gospel in the Xambre church. It influenced the area more than the village itself. The ladies and children from Xambre had remained very faithful, but not as many of the men. But the influence of the church has been greater than just counting statistics.

We had many home services from its very start. Several of our Bible School students and pastors came from this church. Now— partly from our church's influence—even the Catholic Church had 80-100 Home Bible Study groups that meet regularly in the area. This was a dramatic change, for in the early days the Catholic Church didn't want their people to even have—much less, to read or study—a Bible. Many others who had become interested through our personal contact, evangelism campaigns, and tract distributions, ended up in other churches—we praised God for it all.

There is something about the geographical layout of the land that causes frost to hit Xambre very hard—much harder than most areas of Parana. It may be the several rivers that start from springs in this area, or it may be the lay of the land in the rolling countryside and terrain. Almost every year it frosts, and every three or four years the frost is hard enough that much of the coffee first planted never had a harvest.

At first everyone cut the old bushes down so new sprouts would come up again from the roots. But slowly, less and less land remained in coffee. Most of the low ground became pasture for animals. Although coffee had opened up the Frontier in Parana, as time went along more and more cattle came into the area. Cattle required fewer workers as the coffee work had been all done by hand: a big hoe took the place of a plow and cultivator.

The maximum acres of coffee one man could care for was about 10 acres; and with a big family, 20 or 30 acres. Young girls—as well as the boys—worked in the fields. I knew several girls that could do as much work as a man. Before writing a contract, the landlord or owner always asked, "How many *hoes* do you have?"

Looking over the countryside in Xambre now in 1971, it is beautifully green—very little coffee can be seen. It's almost entirely grassland for cattle grazing. A little to the south of this area, the countryside produces soybeans and wheat in rotation—soybeans in the summer; wheat in the winter. Completely mechanized with large tractors and self-propelled combines, fewer workers are needed. Therefore the migration of workers from the more southern area is even greater than from our Xambre area.

The farms surrounding the Xambre area are much smaller, and not practical to mechanize as in other areas. The soil is more of a sandy loam making pasture more practical than grain crops. Pasture controls erosion better, and in dry years the grains produce better in the heavier clay soils.

In the early years when the big farms started, we had regular nightly services in homes of the workers. Then as more churches started, I depended on lay pastors and workers to continue services in the areas. From the beginning we took people along with us in the Jeep to help in the singing and to give their personal testimonies. As time went along, some of these lay pastors continued with the farm services. Sr. Ari de Mello became one of my main helpers.

When Sr. Ari became the caretaker of the Xambre church, they built a home for him. As the work expanded in Perola, Sr. Ari took more and more responsibility for the Xambre work. Shortly after he moved next to the parsonage, we purchased a horse and cart to enable his family to accompany him in holding services in the surrounding area. They had eight active, lovely children whose musical talent became very useful in the services.

By 1965 the church officially considered Sr. Ari their lay pastor. He owned a small farm about one-half mile from their home which provided for their existence. His wife and daughters helped on the farm. In addition, he and his sons worked for other farmers during harvest time: occasionally he did hauling with his cart.

During the first years they had plenty of outside work. As time went on, their opportunities for day labor became less and less. When Sr. Ari officially was placed in charge of the work, the Xambre church helped him financially as he spent most of his time ministering to the people spiritually. Shortly after this, the diminishing work caused many of the people to move on. By 1972 the church received barely enough finances to pay for its expenses—electricity, wax for the floor, and other things.

Then two brothers of Sr. Ari migrated with their families from our area to Curitiba, the state capitol. Since Sr. Ari himself barely made an existence, and their older children who were coming of age couldn't find employment in Xambre, the family made their decision to move to Curitiba.

With this in mind, Sr. Ari went to the capitol to visit his brothers. While there he rented a small house for his family. On his return to Xambre, he asked me to take his family and their few possessions to the city. Because of our close brotherly friendship and his many years of service in the church, I gladly wanted to be of assistance: it was an approximate 1,000 mile round trip to move them to their new home.

The farewell service for Sr. Ari and his family held in the Xambre church stands out as the saddest event we ever had in the church. Like every other special service, the western churches arranged trucks to bring the people together. Sr. Ari was well known and respected by everyone: the church, filled to capacity.

At the conclusion of the service, I called our dear brother and his family to the front for a farewell prayer asking God's blessing on his future ministry. As Sr. Ari faced the audience he began crying like a baby. He had such a great love for every one that he no longer could control his emotions. Several other people cried also, and soon everyone began wiping tears from their eyes. It seemed worse than any death wail emotion that I ever witnessed, and it became the last big church gathering in the area. Without Sr. Ari as lay pastor and caretaker, it was no longer possible to have our big Youth Retreats in Xambre.

Although we sang choruses and hymns as usual during our traveling on the road, I must say, *This was a very sad trip.* Then as I pulled away from their new home after all the farewells, my eyes were so full of tears that I could hardly see to drive.

Sr. Ari de Mello

Jackie adds: *As of March 2006, Sr. Ari is in Heaven reunited with his Pastor Ricardo.*

Sr. Edvin—at age 20—had been a good student in my T.E.E. classes and also a good helper to Sr. Ari de Mello. Sr. Edvin came from a large family of pure Polish blood. Because the family had so much work on the farm, he couldn't attend the Bible School in Maringa. But after his hard day's work—sun-up to sun-down—Sr. Edvin studied at night by a candle or small kerosene lamp. Very seldom did he ever come to class without his lesson well prepared.

It seemed only natural for Sr. Edvin to take charge of the church in Xambre. By walking across the fields instead of using the road, he had approximately three miles to reach the church. Coming down their long lane on his bicycle and using the road, he had a distance of about five miles. Seldom did he miss a service, and I agreed to come to Xambre and help him as much as possible.

The last six months before our furlough in 1973, I drove out every Saturday night, taking along some of our youth to help and encourage the Xambre church. They had charge of their own Sunday school and midweek services.

At the time of our third furlough home—July 1973—both churches in Umuarama were doing very well. Although the exodus of the rural people had greatly affected—directly and indirectly—the commerce of Umuarama, the main encouragement for the church was that more people began coming than were leaving for new environments.

The other four churches—Xambre, Perola, Pindorama, and Fazenda Peroba—were not holding their own: very few came in, and constantly many families moved away.

Pastor Manoel, son-in-law of Sr. Ari and a graduate of our Maringa Bible School, became the official pastor at both Perola and Xambre. By this time a very good bus connection ran between these towns. Lay pastor Jose Rodrigues continued pastoring the Pindorama and Fazenda Peroba churches. Another missionary replaced us while we came back to the States on furlough. We continued to pray much for our churches in western Parana.

Chapter 17

Furlough—1973

At the time of departure for our third furlough home—June 1973—our two sons were living in the States: Rick attended Bible School at Bethany Fellowship, Minneapolis, Minnesota; Ted completed his high school about two months early (April 1973) using the Nebraska course under the supervision of GreenAcre School, and had returned to the U.S.A. ahead of us. Upon arriving in the States, Ted accepted a job as a door-to-door salesman with the Southwest Publishing Company who assigned him to a district in Wheeling, West Virginia.

We stopped in Texas and California to see Jackie's two brothers, then came on to Indiana where we met Rick. Rick traveled with us by car to West Virginia to see Ted, and we had one glorious evening together. Then the five of us—Rick, Anita, Michael, Jackie and I—traveled to Canada to visit the relatives there.

In the fall Ted enrolled at Indiana University South Bend (IUSB), South Bend, Indiana. For his second semester, he transferred to Bethel College, Mishawaka, Indiana, and lived with us as he studied—the only year he ever lived at home while in school. In Brazil all his schooling had taken place at our Mission boarding school—GreenAcre—in Maringa. Ted longed to be back in the dorm for studying and a more social life.

Rick continued to study at Bethany in Minneapolis. We kept in close contact by letters and phone. This communal fellowship group kept him busy, and seemed to be the best thing for him during the time we were out of the country: Bethany Fellowship worked and lived together as one big family.

Michael and Anita attended the local public schools: Anita, a freshman at Northwood High School, Nappanee, Indiana; and Michael, sixth grade at the Harrison Township School in Elkhart County.

The deputation schedule kept me away from home much of the time. I visited many churches in Ohio, Indiana, Michigan, Ontario and Alberta, Canada. Jackie traveled with me on the Canadian trips. We enjoyed the beautiful scenery along the way, and God blessed and helped in my speaking engagements.

The furlough year passed quickly. Soon we began packing for our next term. Our first choice on return to Brazil would have been to go back to the Frontier—Rondonia or the northern Amazon Basin area. However, the Mission felt that much work remained to be done in western Parana. We agreed to return to Umuarama. Everything we purchased we bought with this in mind, and how it could be used there—including our clothing for the winter months.

Before we left Brazil we had electricity from the Government in our home. We also had city water, so we didn't need to worry about this commodity. The week before we left a telephone had been installed in our Mission home, and the asphalt road now extended westward to Umuarama.

Chapter 18

Back in Umuarama—1974

We found many of our Umuarama city streets paved. The city no longer seemed like a Frontier town or area. Our fellow missionaries, Rev. Jim and Jean Coalter and family, along with the church leaders, had done excellent work in our absence. The Chapel church had organized a Home-Coming party for us with a barbeque on the church grounds. Never before had we encountered anything like this on our return to Brazil.

The Youth Group had about 20 teenagers, and our 15-year-old daughter became the center of attraction for the young men. All at once I had to realize our little girl was now a young lady. The welcome became a family affair as the youth brought along their parents and younger siblings, confirming more than ever that we were where God wanted us at this time. We witnessed much spiritual growth among them, too.

At this time the GreenAcre boarding school was no longer an option. But again, God met our need. Another mission had brought in a teacher from the States to teach their children. Graciously they extended an invitation for Anita and Michael to attend their school. For the first time in Brazil, we experienced our children living at home while attending school. Later, because we had adequate space in our home, the teacher even lived with us.

Neither Michael nor Anita had attended any of the Brazilian schools. When Michael entered the seventh grade English class, the (Brazilian) Public School would only accept him at the first grade level. By entering a private Catholic School, he entered at the fourth grade level, and continued his English correspondence courses at home. The second year we realized the load had become too difficult for him to continue with both school systems, and he handled all his studies by correspondence.

The influence of our children greatly helped bring other families into the church. They made contacts that we couldn't have made, and many of their friends began attending our Chapel church. As a part of the Young People's Group, their participation made our ministry more effective.

Anita finished her high school in English at the Bethany Missionary Fellowship Children's School. Their school was located in Altonia, Parana, so she was able to come home every weekend.

As Umuarama developed into the business and cultural center of western Parana, the Public School system improved. Almost everyone under 30 years of age had enrolled in a school somewhere. Some schools ran three or four sessions a day. Many opened their doors at 7:00 a.m. and did not lock up until midnight. They had an entirely new student body every three to four hours, including a change of teachers. They offered courses up to a Junior College level in several fields of study. Adults also took courses, learning to read and write.

Now our church programs had to adjust to the school systems. Special meetings, Retreats, and other services needed to be planned according to school holidays and vacation times. Since most of our youth and some of the adults attended evening classes, the midweek services had only children and very few adults. The children attended classes in the morning or afternoon: most of our church youth worked during the day and took classes at night.

Church still continued to be the center of activity for most of our youth. They made new friends at school and brought many of them along to our activities—generally coming in groups. The youth had grown up in a culture where parents (or younger brothers and sisters) traditionally chaperoned their daughters until married. Some continued this practice, and in no way did we try to change the custom.

Many times we had parties and gatherings of the Youth at our home. Most of these get-togethers were held after the evening service, and often became late—after the city's curfew hours. Night guards patrolled the streets, but parents didn't worry when they knew their children were at our home. But because of the late hour, an adult always accompanied them to their home. Usually we had too many to take in our Mission vehicle. However, an active Youth Group attracts more attention (and probably protection) when they walk together. We praise God how He blessed the Chapel in Umuarama.

The Lord also blessed the Vila church. Gustavo graduated from the Bethany Bible School in November 1974. Often he had come to help, and after his graduation the Lord led him to work in the Vila church. The apartment at the back of the church had been rebuilt, and a bathroom installed—equipped with running water.

Cleber and Joan Lacerda with their daughter soon moved back to Umuarama and also helped in the Vila work—Joan, the daughter of Norm and Betty Charles, and Cleber is the son of Sr. Valdemar, one of our most faithful lay workers since 1958.

The Vila church received help from the Chapel youth and adults, and the two churches took care of the financial support of their young pastor—Gustavo.

In January 1975 the Mission sent Gerald Steele and his family to help in the Umuarama area. As new missionaries, they had just finished their Language School training program, and would be working among the other four western churches from which many people continued to migrate. I didn't have much time to help these western churches.

Immediately on returning to Umuarama I resumed teaching the T.E.E. classes for lay pastors and church leaders—eight in the first classes of 1974. These classes were a real challenge as I knew the students would be using the lesson in their church the following Sunday.

The Fazenda Peroba church continued to become weaker. It became difficult for Pastor Jose Rodrigues to adequately pastor both Pindorama and Peroba. Almost all of the Christians had moved off the farm, and from the neighborhood—only four active members remained.

Attempting to help Peroba, every other week I took some of our youth from the Chapel church to hold services. Attendance picked up. But the people came for entertainment rather than to worship, and came only on the weeks that we brought the young people. But the four members continued to meet together regularly for prayer and Bible study.

The Vila church in Umuarama needed a larger building. At my recommendation the National Church approved the dismantling of the Peroba farm church to be rebuilt in Umuarama: the Peroba farm group then made a small chapel in the building which had been the caretaker's home. But now Umuarama had city codes in place. We needed to obtain permission from the authorities for this move—to rebuild the (Peroba) farm church inside the city limits.

Umuarama had passed an ordinance requiring all future public buildings to be built of brick—including churches. Since most of the homes in our area were of wood construction, they granted us permission, but required an engineer to supervise the details of the construction.

Dismantling the 8 x 16 meter building and rebuilding it to an 8 x 12 meter building was no small job. Actually it took more than twice the work of building with new lumber. We had the church, but very little finances.

Since I had moved this same church at the farm, it seemed only logical that I should supervise its reconstruction again. Volunteer labor came from the churches and pastors—Gerald Steele and Gustavo of the Vila as well as Sr. Jose Rodrigues—gave of their time and energy to help. The job began in November, and we dedicated the church—uncompleted—in February.

Spring came and went. The end of the summer vacation period approached, and soon the students would be back in their evening classes again. We went ahead with our special week of services with the ceiling and painting incomplete. The old boards and framework didn't look very beautiful. In fact, its looks became very effective in taking offerings to help finish the building, but the *looks* certainly didn't hurt the *spirit* of the meetings.

The first night every seat was filled before the service started. Five minutes after the meeting began no standing room remained—not even in the aisles. Many looked in through the windows. Although the church held only 200, more than 300 were present. The meeting lasted from one Sunday through to the next Sunday with an average of more than 200 each night.

Several excellent Brazilian Bible teachers and evangelists preached: the Lord led me to speak one evening. In addition, each night we used a religious film. The Chapel youth choir sang in every service as well as during the time for singing and praise testimonies. Nearly every night people came forward to seek God's help for healings, salvation, and some individuals were released of demon possession in these services. It was a real harvest time for the many years of faithful ministry in the Vila church.

It took another month after the dedication to finish the construction. The schools were back in session, and we had less volunteer help. But if we had waited to have the dedication after the church was entirely completed, our crowds would have been much smaller because of the night school sessions. Although the old church building—remodeled—made a nice parsonage, we still used the large front living room as a Sunday school classroom.

The western churches looked very discouraging. They needed all the help they could get. Since both the Chapel and Vila churches were going very well, I put Pastor Gustavo and his new wife in charge of the Vila church, and our fellow missionary, Gerald Steele, took over the Chapel.

Our family then moved—March 1976—into a nice home on the Fazenda Santa Fe farm. We had held close fellowship with the personnel that managed Santa Fe; had been in their homes often to visit, or for lunch; and they often dropped in to see us regardless of the time of day. From this farm we could drive to any of the four churches within a half an hour. We did not plan, or intend, to pastor any one of the churches—only encourage their leaders. Also, from here I could maintain fairly close contact with these pastors and lay leaders through my T.E.E. classes.

However, just previous to our move to the Santa Fe farm, the pastor in Perola moved almost 200 kilometers (125 miles) east to pastor a work in Apucarama. Another of my T.E.E. students, a lay pastor, took his place and became the pastor at Perola.

About the same time Sr. Jose Rodrigues moved with his family from Pindorama to Xambre to be closer to the public school where their children attended. This move created enthusiasm that encouraged the church in Xambre, and also enabled Sr. Jose to continue his own schooling. Officially he remained the pastor of the Pindorama, Fazenda Peroba, and Xambre churches.

Because of Sr. Jose's heavy schedule, we already were helping (March 1976) at the Peroba farm church, and sometimes in Pindorama.

Then shortly after our March 1976 move, Pastor Jose and his family moved to the state capitol, Curitiba, and the lay worker at Perola—unable to find employment—moved to Cruzeiro de Oeste. So, once again, I had the responsibility as pastor of *all four* churches: no easy job on the constantly moving, and always migrating Frontiers.

Previously when I had this responsibility, the churches were new, growing, and the members of the church helped. But now almost all of the families I had known and depended on had moved to new environments. I had a heavy load to try to encourage and strengthen the remaining Christians, training them to take over the responsibilities.

I became aware that our Bible School graduates seemed more interested in their own pastoral positions rather than training their lay persons as teachers and workers. But the Lord helped us through it all. Jackie could not go with me to some of these services as she was home-schooling Michael. But the two children often accompanied me and helped. Very seldom did I have a service by myself.

The last six months—December 15, 1976 through June 1977—the Chapel at Umuarama requested that we should pastor that work: the Steele family had gone home on furlough.

At first I didn't see how we could possibly consider their request. However, our children—Anita and Michael—pleaded for us to accept the invitation because they had so many friends in the church, and agreed to continue helping in the services of *all* the churches.

It became a privilege and refreshing experience to again give assistance to this active growing Chapel church. When I couldn't get to the western churches because of rain and mud, the people helped by taking charge of their own services.

Chapter 19

More Trips North

Shortly after our arrival in Brazil for our fourth term—July 1974—the National Church decided that Pastor Mario Miki, our National leader, and I should visit our Christians who had moved on into the Frontier territory of Rondonia, Mato Grosso. Traveling by bus and with good connections, we made the trip in three days. This included a layover of several hours in Cuiaba—about the half-way mark—and dirt roads the rest of the way.

The bus terminal in Cuiaba reminded me of Maringa 15 years earlier—completely filled with people with all their earthly possessions. Many people stood around waiting, others had baggage scattered all over the place, and the smaller children either sat or slept on blankets. Already many of these people had spent most of their money for the trip north and could not afford a hotel. Without money some families needed to stay at the terminal a week or more during the rains before getting a bus to complete the trip to their destination.

We arrived about 7:00 a.m. The children were covered with old tattered blankets that looked like rags: their mattresses were burlap bags containing all their earthly belongings. That morning we counted 50-75 children who had spent the night on the sidewalk in front of the bus station under its extended roof—their only protection from the early morning mist.

Our bus arrived more than an hour late, but soon we were roaring westward toward Porto Velho, a 36 hour run when the roads are in top shape. Two drivers switched off as ticket collector, salesman, and a driving team. We stopped every two or three hours for coffee, lunch, fuel, and a quick motor checkup while another mechanic quickly examined the tires. Several times on the trip we had a half hour stop/delay to adjust the brakes, and other things. Late at night and without any light in the small towns, the mechanic checked things by flashlight.

During the day we made poor time: the bus stopped for anyone along the road. For parts of the trip, people stood in the aisle. At night children slept on the floor. We carried so much baggage that some of it had to be tied on top of the bus, secured by a canvas placed over it. Several times when the bus hit a hole in the road, suitcases from the baggage rack above our heads fell down on the passengers.

Always there was the need for the passengers to stretch their legs and go to the bathroom. During the early morning hour stops, the driver announced that the ladies were to get out first, and then the men: of course the bathroom was right in the middle of the road. Getting out, we had to be careful not to step on the children sleeping on the floor of the aisle.

After traveling together on the bus for a period of time we got to know one another quite well. It didn't take long until the passengers began calling Sr. Mario and I "the Japanese and American pastors." With interest we visited and learned the backgrounds of the various families, and listened to their expectations, confidence and hope, in the new venture which lay ahead in *the North.*

We explained to them that their greatest hope was in Christ—they needed Him to help them and protect them on the Frontier. They all accepted the Gospel tracts we constantly handed to each new person as they boarded the bus. I played the tapes of the new songs and praise choruses we brought along to teach our people in the north what we were learning in our churches back home. They enjoyed the music. At one of the coffee stops I asked a man if he would watch my cassette recorder while I left the bus. He said, "Sure, may I listen to it, too?"

The hot sun made the inside of the bus like an oven. The fresh air coming in through the windows was as warm as the temperature outside—around 100 degrees. Everyone was hot and sweaty. Between bus stops they passed around a big two-gallon plastic jug of water and a cup from which to drink. Mario took a drink—said it was "good", so I took a drink.

A short time later we stopped at a small stream. Someone grabbed and filled the jug again with water. The water I drank may have been from another stream. But God protected us. Neither Sr. Mario nor I became sick during the entire trip. Several of the children aboard had motion sickness during the extreme heat of the day, caused partly by of the rough roads. At the next stop someone always cleaned up the mess with fresh water and a mop.

As we approached Vila Rondonia—about four hours from the end of the line—many of the passengers began leaving the bus at small towns along the way. We picked up new homesteaders who were going into the villages for their supplies. Usually they carried a 60 kilo (120 lb.) sack of rice, beans, or other produce to trade at the General Store for sugar, salt, or other needs including medicine. Vila Rondonia—one of the first settlements for homesteaders in the territory—already had more than 20,000 inhabitants.

After a shower, lunch, and a short rest in a hotel, we were ready to visit our people in the area. We hired a Jeep-taxi to take us out to their homes.

On arrival the families insisted that we stay with them: we sent the taxi back to town. Staying in their homes gave us more time to visit—both late into the night and early in the mornings. Each evening we gathered in a different home for a service, refreshments, and more conversation. They enjoyed learning the new songs that we brought—taped from the Chapel services.

Many of the HCJB radio listeners recognized Pastor Mario's voice and felt they knew him personally after listening on a regular basis to the Mission tapes sent to Quito, Ecuador. The Gospel messages had been beamed back into Brazil with Pastor Mario's voice, and his voice had become very familiar to this area. Now our follow up was reaping souls into the Kingdom.

Pastor Mario Miki

A small transistor radio is one of the first items the people purchase after their first harvest. The best station to pick up is HCJB from Quito. Even after the batteries are too weak to pick up other Brazilian stations, HCJB comes in very good. Many people have been helped through the evangelical programming and good music coming from this station. Every active church in the north is seeing 40%-50% increase per year.

This week went too fast. Our trip had been to encourage and strengthen the Christians in the area. We felt successfully rewarded. The taxi-pickup-truck that made regular runs between several of the villages picked us up and took us back to town.

We had good connections coming home. It gave us time for prayer and reflection: my eyes filled with tears of compassion for those we left behind with so many needs and going through so much suffering and hardships. However, we were very tired at the end of our first day of traveling.

As we crossed the street in the downtown section of Vila Rondonia one of the local trucks with a PA system drove past advertising a sale in a nearby store. Suddenly a voice broke into the dialogue, "Welcome to Rondonia, Pastor Ricardo!"

The greeting came from a man who had been a mechanic in Xambre 13 years earlier. In passing he recognized us and gave us this unique welcome. He was only one of many in the area that we had not seen for a very long time. In fact, I now knew more people in this area than in the area of Xambre, Perola, and Umuarama where we had spent our entire missionary life.

Porto Velho—the capitol of the territory—is the old rubber export town on the Madeira River, a branch of the Amazon River. In high tide the ocean freighters can come into this port where large storage buildings hold supplies waiting for the high tides. We wanted to obtain more information from the government officials, and visit this old city which was supposed to be only a four hour bus ride.

But soon after leaving Rondonia our bus had a flat tire. They always check the tires at each stop, but with all the bad roads it is a wonder the tires hold up as well as they do. When they took off the inside dual, somehow they broke the brake line completely off. Without a way to repair it on the road, they drove a sharp stick into the brake line. Needless to say, we didn't have very good brakes.

Then at the bus stop in the village of Ouro Preto we saw some of the sickest people that I have ever seen—malaria, hepatitis, parasites, and other tropical diseases. One young man with his family laid waiting for our bus to take him to a government hospital in Porto Velho: so sick that he couldn't speak anymore. I counseled his father that the son would never make the trip, and told him to take his son back to the hospital in Vila Rondonia. He replied that he had no money, and after several days he finally received written permission from the government official that his way would be paid to the hospital as well as the hospital costs incurred.

At the next stop it took an hour to repair the tire and get it mounted back on the bus. During this waiting period the young man died *inside* the bus. Of course, the police officials had to be called to the scene. Then the mother of the lad became hysterical with her crying and wailing. She wondered why God had brought her family out to "...this green hell."

This young man was the second or third child that this couple had lost on the Frontier, and other family members were at home, sick. Here they sat without money, couldn't continue on the bus, and had no way to get home. Pastor Mario and I took up an offering among the passengers to rent a taxi to take the parents back home.

Loaded up again, our bus almost flew down the road. As we came over the crest of a hill and saw a long downgrade ahead, we could see another bus sitting in the middle of the road at the edge of a narrow bridge. Our driver did everything he could to stop our bus with the stick still stuck in the broken brake line. By downshifting, he managed to slow the bus. The brakes helped a little. But almost everyone realized that we could not avoid this accident.

Since I sat in the second seat from the front door, I braced myself and ducked my head just before we crashed into the back of the other bus. When we hit, the windshield on the right side exploded. Flying glass cut quite badly an arm and the entire leg of the lady in front of me. When the bus finally stopped, she exclaimed, "Oh, my God! I'm dying, too!"

The bus carried a big First-Aid kit. A passenger who worked in a drugstore—a male nurse—cleaned and dressed her wounds. Someone swept away the broken glass.

The previous night a big cattle truck had missed the bridge and ran into the ravine. The bus in front of us had stopped to check on the accident in an effort to help, if they could.

Mechanically, the accident didn't bother us for the rest of the two-hour trip. We continued to speed along the road at the same speed. Dust, insects, and all, came right through the open windshield. We were all wind-blown and dirty by the time we pulled into the bus station in Porto Velho.

I told the taxi driver that Mario and I wanted a fairly nice hotel. He took us to the Shelton Hotel. Here we had air conditioning and even a telephone in our room. A swimming pool helped us to relax and enjoy some therapeutic exercise. After such a trip, this paradise hotel seemed impossible to believe.

After showering, getting into fresh clothes, and enjoying an excellent dinner, I phoned Jackie in Umuarama—about 3000 kilometers (1875 miles) away—via satellite connection. It was so good to hear her voice, and to be able to tell her we were headed home. The next day we caught the evening bus going south.

With fewer people along the road at night and no breakdowns, this bus made much better time. Because this road—the only road—going through this big territory is such a rugged run, they aim to replace the bus at least every two years.

Many trails lead off from this road to the new farms being cut out of the jungle. Government officials marked off the lots along these new trails by driving stakes on both sides of the future roads. Each new farm is one-half kilometer by two kilometers—about 250 acres. Then the officials go another four kilometers and mark off the next lots in the same way.

When the new homesteaders finally cut down their lot and get it under cultivation, the government will come back again and drive the stakes for the back side of the lots. But one of the problems is that people are coming in so fast that the government officials can't mark out the lots fast enough. Many families are going beyond the marked plots—as squatters—who will then have first rights to the land.

There is a plan to pay for the lots in 20 years. At the same time the homesteaders must live on their own land and begin to develop it. As they develop their land, they can go to the bank and get a loan to help them continue to develop their plot. So in reality, with the benefits that the government is doing along with the tremendous 40%-50% inflation per year and low interest loans, the government is actually paying these poorer people to develop their own land.

The suffering from diseases and the injuries received in cutting down the jungle are unbelievable. Malaria and hepatitis are in epidemic stages. It is known that even the monkeys had malaria before man began to infiltrate the jungle. Every time I visited up there the statistics had grown worse. The government is trying to help, but so many people are coming into the area that the census statistics are very inaccurate.

The officials do have the names of all the new owners. But since there is so much work by hand involved, some owners have taken in their entire family—uncles, aunts, grandparents, and others—under one name, the owner's name, for each plot. There may be 20 people or more living and working on the site under one name.

Chain saws are dangerous and a hazard in the jungle. The vines hold and bind the trees together. Often several trees must be cut before *any* tree will fall. A man skilled with a chain saw would hesitate before tackling a job such as this. But as soon as they receive their clearance for a loan, the new homesteaders want saws to help them clear the land. Most are inexperienced with the chain saw, and many are injured or killed by falling limbs and trees. Very few families escape having several deaths within their family after migrating to the Frontier.

The area is very, very ripe for evangelism. Families previously uninterested in the Gospel before moving to the Frontier now need emotional, physical, and spiritual help because of their sufferings due to illnesses, injuries, and deaths within their families and community. Almost every service has seekers at the altar. *It is a field ripe for harvest.*

Back home, we put together a nice slide presentation of our trip. The churches and people were very interested in the Frontier work. One of these services we held in a home close to our Peroba farm church. Almost all of the neighbors came, and nearly everyone had some kind of a plan to move to the Frontier. They came—not for spiritual reasons—only for the information, and to hear the reports from those who had gone to the northern Frontier.

These northern pioneers who survive the hardships are making good money—more money than they had after many years of work in Parana where most of the workers are day-workers who have never handled much money. But the pioneers do not tell of the extreme hardships, or any of the sufferings experienced on the Frontier.

As elsewhere, most suffering comes from overwork, unsanitary conditions, and the lack of prevention in both situations. In some areas the people rest during the heat of the day: *a siesta*. In Manaus and Belem many banks and businesses close for a couple hours during mid-day, and remain open in the evening until 8:00 or 9:00. But the hard working farmers of Parana try to work from sun-up until dark, and become so exhausted from the extreme heat that they retain very little resistance against diseases.

Migration holds the opportunity to own a farm. We felt the need to pray much—daily, and in every service—for these Frontiersmen: may they find their needs met in Christ our Savior while they are so open to the Gospel.

Return Trip: About a year later, the Brazilian National Church sent a young couple who recently graduated from the Bible School— Sr. Antonio Ramos and his wife Marlene—to pastor our church in the Vila Rondonia area. Later Sr. Antonio petitioned the National Church for me to come and introduce them to the believers scattered throughout the Northern area who had formerly attended our churches in western Parana. While there, the National Church wanted me to help build a parsonage for the young couple.

I agreed to go north if we could go as a family: Jackie, Anita and Michael, too. At this time the Mission didn't have any VW bus in tip-top shape. We loaded our own VW bus to capacity with building materials which could be purchased for much less in our area than at the Frontier. We even had the kitchen sink with us. The Lord held our bus together as it bounced over those rough roads.

Before arriving back home we had to purchase a complete set of tires. Even the battery gave out, and we drove hundreds of miles before we could buy another one. The spark became so weak that we could hardly make it up many of the long hills. But we made good time going downhill. Then one day we didn't cover very many miles—the vehicle just couldn't run right. But marvelously, God kept that old bus running.

One night (up north) we took a full load of people out to a home service. On the way back I thought one tire made some noise. When I checked the next morning I found that more than half of the tread had pealed off: we had come home on bare threads. All the tires had tubes—meaning this tire was less than half the thickness of the inner tube. Including the passengers, we had carried almost a ton of weight. Only God brought us home safely over that rugged rough trail—often called "the onca trail" as many oncas had been seen regularly in the area.

One term I had taught a Monday night Bible lesson at a Bible School in Cianorte. So now the church leaders here in the city called me "the Professor of the Bible", and the church filled to capacity. Immediately other churches invited me to teach Bible studies in their churches.

About six months previous to our trip, Jackie and Cidinha (a graduate of Maringa B.S.) had translated Bill Gaither's song *The Family of God* into Portuguese. It made an excellent trio for Jackie, Michael, and Anita to sing, and a wonderful introduction to each Bible Study by creating an atmosphere of fellowship. Everybody loved the hymn, and soon everyone knew the song by memory.

One contact lead to another, and families began coming who had never attended our churches in the south—the Western Parana churches. Finally, we had to turn down invitations for meetings in order to find time to talk to and care for the people who came to meet with us.

In the center of town we met an older lady from Xambre—the old baker's wife—whose family had been among the first people that came to live in Xambre: a strong Catholic family. Jackie delivered one of their children. Since that time they always called the babe she delivered "our American daughter."

Not long after moving up here, her husband (the baker) died. One of her sons that I remembered as a little boy in Xambre became a driver of one of the many buses. This dear elderly mother hugged us and shed tears at seeing us: we belonged to her as "family". We experienced many reunions such as this. I hardly found time to organize the building of the parsonage.

There had been a mix-up in the money being sent from our National Church to build the parsonage. So we were able to plan a trip to see a family from "the south" — *remember Sr. Joao (John) Chagas from Xambre?*

We drove back in the jungle as far as our vehicle would go. Then we locked everything up tightly and walked along a jungle trail for more than a half an hour before we reached a cleared portion of land. There stood two houses where our friends lived. What a greeting we received from Sr. Joao & Maura, Sr. Amilton & Maria and the children. We had a service with them that evening and stayed overnight. Sr. Amilton & Maria eventually lost three of their children on the Frontier.

Jackie and I slept on a primitive bed made of scrap-wood lined with a corn husk mattress. Anita slept on a similar bed, and Michael hung a hammock in the storeroom. It was interesting — maybe even terrifying — for our children to go to sleep to the noise of mice and insects in the thatched roof above our heads. Again, God was with us. It meant so much to them to have us visit, and we felt privileged to be with them.

We spent most of that month teaching, visiting, and planning construction. Eventually the money arrived, and the lumber and materials were delivered.

A carpenter — a young man from Perola — who helped build the Perola church had been contracted to build the parsonage. In Perola I saw his potential and had encouraged him to make construction his trade. He not only called me his spiritual father, but also considered me the teacher of his profession. Now he had eight children, and they all called us their "grandparents".

We arranged to extend an electric wire from the other side of the block to have power on the construction site. With the power saw and drill I could cut the lumber and drill holes for the nails as fast as the carpenter could mark it. By the end of the week we had the siding and roof on the framework. Now the young carpenter and pastor could finish the house without my assistance. Although it would have been so easy to stay on in this work for God, we soon had to head for home again.

As a family we had become close to the people. They confided even deeper sufferings and hardships than we had heard on previous trips: sufferings and hardships that only God could bring them through.

One large family had been here in the north only a few months before losing their 21 year old son to malaria, and then their 22 year old son-in-law died as a result of a portion of a tree falling on him.

After cutting a couple trees loose from their base, suddenly the vines holding them broke and let them all fall — this is the jungle. A few seconds later a big limb broke off another tree also entangled in the same vines: the limb fell on him, causing his death.

In the south this family never had an interest in religion. During our stay in the north, the family didn't miss even one service. Daily and nightly we came across situations like this: while going through difficult circumstances people are much more open for God's help.

The young pastors in this area have had very little chance for any formal Bible school. They need more training in the Word to be better equipped as pastors to meet the many needs presented.

Chapter 20

Culture Shock

To most of us the words "culture shock" immediately cause us to think of arriving in a foreign country, seeing and hearing things unfamiliar to our own life.

In preparing for overseas missionary service we read and study regarding the country to which we are going. In many ways we are prepared for what we will see. Even so, many things are different than expected. The main difficulty is being unable to converse freely in the language of the people. In time, this is no longer a problem as we learn the language and the Lord helps us in all the adjustments.

To us, the greater shock came each furlough on our return to the U.S.A.: each visit back became a greater shock. The language used and spoken here in the homeland; the standards of dress and living; and the whole concept of things that should be of most importance in the lives of Christians had changed: it all had changed.

As a child my life had been sheltered from worldly things. Our community perhaps was more sheltered. The influence of Godly preachers ranked high in our great country. We were taught to respect and obey authority. What father said was not to be questioned, and this gave us a good beginning in respecting other authorities as we grew up. The Bible clearly teaches submission to authority: Romans 13:1 ...*Let every soul be subject unto the higher powers. For there is no power but of God; the powers that be are ordained of God ....* We were taught to love your neighbors: Matthew 19:19b ...*Thou shalt love thy neighbor as thyself....*

In the days of my youth the community spirit at threshing time and other times kept the people in a close fellowship. Neighbors cared what happened to a friend, and lent a helping hand with chores around the farm and barnyard. Sin was present, but not out in open view, or as unashamedly as it is now.

In these days sin is flagrantly displayed on many TV programs, right within most homes. Things previously considered unfit to be seen anywhere are now regularly watched in homes—fightings, murders, drunkenness, obscene language, illicit sex, nudeness, and much more: you may complete the sentence.

Coming back home to the U.S.A. we see changed interests: the school and other outside activities have taken so much of our young people's time that there is no time or energy left for home-life. In the rush of everything, family altars (a time for devotions and prayer) which make the foundation for the beginning of a child's life to be lived for Christ, are a thing of the past.

As the child is taught at home, then at church and with a salvation experience, he or she will be better able to stand strong in their faith while attending public school. But when school activities are first, and no time remains for Christ or the home, the story is much different.

The changes we have seen when coming back home grieve us. The total impact of the public school is against the basic Bible teachings and the standards of Christian homes. We praise God for the Christian school teachers that still stand firm, but the books and the laws prohibit them from taking a Christian stand in most situations. Evolutionary theories are taught as almost fact rather than theory: at the same time the teacher/professor is prohibited from teaching Biblical history which is even scorned by most administrators in the Education Departments. Textbooks are written with a humanitarian viewpoint and have completely neglected the impact of Christian mission influences in other parts of the world. Yet at the same time the textbooks greatly praise the communist and socialist influences in helping backward nations, and ignore the fact that most of the early hospitals and education systems were started by mission groups from other countries.

The total education system is far from being God-centered and God-ordained. Almost everything the Bible and church have taught is being questioned and much is rejected. This lack of respect for God, parental authority, and submission to *any* authority abounds.

Most schools in our democratic system are run almost completely by the students. This is against the theocratic teaching of the Bible.

Participating in sports of all kinds, or watching such events, has become a dominant part of our culture. I have always enjoyed sports—for pleasure in my leisure time—but my devotions and church activities come first. On our missionary tours I see the standards have changed. If there is a game of football or basketball at the local high school, it would be best to cancel church meetings—very few will show up for a Missionary Convention, or service.

There are more and more professional teams: the stadiums are getting bigger and better while our churches are struggling to hold their own with enough money to meet their budget. In these days most Christian youth know more professional ball players by name than Bible characters. This shows that most Christian youth are on a spiritual starvation diet: sports are not wrong when kept in their proper perspectives.

It should be the natural thing within our homes to see the child grow up and become active in their local church. A healthy church should be on the increase without the outreach programs and evangelistic services. Sad to say many older (senior citizen age) Christians have become so legalistic that there is no love and consideration remaining to attract the youth.

God told Peter three times to ...*feed my sheep....* As sheep are fed they reproduce. As Christians should show love and caring among the family of God and in the church, our youth should not have to wander from the fold to graze on love and recognition. The fruit of the spirit should be very evident in the lives of spirit-filled Christians.

A spiritual renewal is sweeping across America, they say. But in comparison it touches only the minority of the population. So greatly are the masses involved in spectatoritis and materialism, they don't have time to listen for the voice of God, or read His Word.

Christian TV carries some excellent programs featuring outstanding pastors, evangelists, Faith healers, Bible Schools, Christian Colleges and Seminaries. We praise God for this, but *a great work still remains to be done through God's people.*

This means that the harvest field is not only in other countries, it's the whole world—including America. We have a burden for Brazil as we see it also fast becoming materialistic in many ways. But as we come home and see the situation here in the States, our hearts are burdened for our homeland as well.

A complete and irrevocable return to God and the Bible is the only answer for our self-ridden, leisure-loving, self-centered, materialistic world. May God use us as Christian people to be His witnesses and to manifest His Spirit by showing His love to all mankind—everywhere.

Chapter 21

Impact of the Missionary Church

The Impact of the Missionary Church in Brazil is much greater than statistics or the records indicate. Through our Mission Bible Bookstore at Maringa and HCJB Radio ministry we have reached and strengthened ALL DENOMINATIONS. A very small percentage of our sales of Bibles, records, and religious books were to our own church people. The TV and Radio reach all who tune in from the listening areas. The many letters we receive indicate an excellent listening audience from many denominations as HCJB beams its way into Brazil.

Our own ministry has been mostly in a small area within a radius of about 40 miles. But the migration of our converts to many other parts of Brazil greatly spread the impact of our work and ministry into these other areas.

Rondonia, about 3000 kilometers from Xambre, received people who have migrated from almost every part of Brazil as well as those from our area. While visiting out in the jungle in Rondonia—more than 30 miles from the main road—a man came up to us saying he had been in one of our farm services close to the town of Ipora, in Parana. Although we seldom went there, we always had large crowds at the Ipora farm. We never got to know this man or become acquainted with all the people who attended our services. This was the situation in many of the farm services during the early years.

Since meeting this man, we learned that he gave his heart to the Lord, and our converts from the Xambre area confirmed that he attends services regularly in their homes.

Our state capitol, Curitiba, became home to many of our people. One of our members—Sr. Ari de Mello, my helper and a lay-pastor at Xambre—continues to hold regular services in his home in Curitiba.

Missionaries handle much official paperwork as they prepare for travel between countries. One of the times when we went by bus to Curitiba to get our papers in order, I had just stepped off the bus in that huge terminal when a young man walked up calling me by name. I couldn't remember him.

About 15 years ago he had been in our Sunday school in Xambre. At only seven years of age, he often sang special songs with his parents. Now at age 22, he had a wife and two children. On this particular day he was moving from a town in the southern part of Parana into Curitiba where he had found a job as a carpenter. He had rented a small house and was going back to get his family. Joyfully, I gave him news of his family back in western Parana. Then I gave him the address of Sr. Ari de Mello and encouraged him to make contact with Sr. Ari to attend the services here in Curitiba.

Chapter 22

Flight Home—1977

Rio de Janeiro—the old capitol of Brazil—is a beautiful scenic city often visited by travelers. Anita and Michael, our two youngest children, had been too young to remember seeing the city some years earlier when we passed through. We planned our flight back to the U.S.A. from "Rio" to allow us a few days there before leaving for our furlough home.

On our way to Rio we visited two of our Christian families. One family was a young pastor and his wife who had graduated from our Bible School and became house parents—in charge of an orphanage. We stayed overnight in their home and had a wonderful visit getting reacquainted.

The second family had moved from our area and became active in a Presbyterian church as our Mission didn't have a church near them. Their experience in Xambre made them well qualified to help in church work: he was their lay pastor. We visited several hours into the night. They gave us their beds, but we didn't use them very long. What a delight to have such sweet fellowship with fellow Christians.

On to Rio de Janeiro with its magnificent sights: Copacabana Beach, Sugar Loaf Mountain, Christ the Redeemer (statue) on Mount Corcovado, many more beaches, the large football stadium, the old Imperial Buildings, and many more interesting sights.

Then one day as we walked in the downtown area, a young man grabbed me by the arm saying, "What are you doing in Rio, Pastor Ricardo?"

I looked, and sure enough—I knew him—Sr. Mario Cezar—yes, I remembered him! About 12 years ago he ran off with our maid: the way a young couple forces their parents to consent to their marriage. It is not a commendable manner of handling the issue, of course, but done by many young couples whose parents do not consent to their marriage. It forces the situation on their parents very effectively.

Well, afterwards Sr. Mario straightened himself out spiritually, and became one of my best students in the T.E.E. classes. After they moved away, we lost track of them. Now at this meeting he gave me the good news that he had a small pastorate and is attending a seminary while working part time to support his family: his wife and family are well, and they are serving the Lord. Praise God for this encounter.

As we left Brazil we could even thank the Lord for inflation that made many hotels too expensive to stay in. It had forced us to carry along our sleeping bags and stay with friends. Our fellowship with friends made the trip so much more enjoyable. We witnessed the Lord blessing each one in their home and surroundings. Our home always had been kept open to our friends—now their home opened wide for us with such sweet fellowship.

The Love of God is spread in many, many ways. We thank Him for the privilege of having a tiny part in the spreading of His wonderful Gospel, and being ...

Called According to His Purpose,

Dick

The Obituary
Of
Rev. Richard Ummel

Wakarusa—the Rev. Richard Ummel (56) of 61955 CR 7 South (of Elkhart), died Tuesday evening, September 8 1981, at the home of a friend, Dan King, on CR 32, where he was visiting. He apparently suffered a heart attack. He was recovering from a stroke he suffered about six weeks ago.

He was born August 15, 1925, in Harrison Township, Elkhart County to Edward and Edith (Anglemyer) Ummel. He married Jacquelyn E. McReynolds on August 22, 1952, in Owen Sound, Ontario, Canada. She survives along with one daughter, Miss Anita Ummel, Puerto Rico, and three sons: Richard, Jr., Minneapolis; T. Edward Ummel, Argos; and Michael, at home; two grandchildren; his mother, Edith Ummel, Columbia City; and five brothers: Robert, Rolling Prairie; Eldon, Syracuse; Herbert, Elkhart; Stanley, Fremont; and Max, Rochester; and four sisters: Carol Hines, Fort Wayne; Lois Knouff, St. Louis, Mo.; Joan Kirkham, Greencastle; and Phyllis Swick, Columbia City.

Friends may call from 2:00-8:00 p.m. Thursday at the Lienhart Funeral Home in Wakarusa. His body will lie in state for one hour prior to services at 2:00 p.m. Friday at the Bethel Missionary Church. Burial will be in the Yellow Creek Union cemetery.

Richard moved to the area from Claypool in 1951; he served as a missionary in Brazil under the United Missionary Society of the Missionary Church from 1956-1978, in charge of church planting.

Memorials may be given to the Bethel Missionary church, designated for overseas mission work.

Dates to Remember

Dick & Jackie	**Their Children**

Wedding in Canada:
August 22, 1952

Birth: Rick   June 28, 1953
Birth: Ted   March 6, 1955

To Brazil: August 1956
Home to USA: January 1957
Returned to Brazil: August 1957

Birth: Anita   March 10, 1959

Home to USA: April 1962

Birth: Michael   June 5, 1962

Returned to Brazil: June 1963
Home to USA: June 1967
Leave of Absence: 1968-69

Remodeled the Schoolhouse:
1968-69

Returned to Brazil: July 1969

Rick stayed in US: 1969
Graduated HS: 1971
Graduated Bethany Fellowship:
1974
Married: 8-22-75

Home to USA: July 1973

Ted graduated HS: 1973
Graduated Bethel College 1977
Married: 6-10-78
Graduated Valparaiso
University
School of Law: 1980

Returned to Brazil: July 1974

Anita graduated HS: 1977
Graduated Bethany Fellowship:
1983
Married: 12-16-89

Michael graduated HS: 1980
Graduated Bethel College:
1984
Married: 8-4-84

Home to USA: May 1977

Dick became Ill: Fall 1978
Awoke in his Heavenly Home:
9-8-1981
Jackie returned to Brazil: 1984

To God Be the Glory
For
The Calling According to His Purpose

Rick's Family
Rick, Rachel, Ryan, Vikki

Ted's Family
Tracy, Brenda, Ted, Phillip

Anita's (Riquelme) Family
Michelle, Ricardo, Roger,
Anita, Miguel

Michael's Family
Jeremy,
Michael w/Madelyn Joy,
Alexis, Joanne

The Family
Front L-R: Brenda, Tracy, Ted, Miguel, Phillip, Michelle,
Alexis, Jeremy
Back L-R: Rachel (Brown), Jackie, Matt Brown w/Tori, Ricardo,
Anita, Roger, Ryan, Vikki, Joanne, Michael

Coming up to Date:

Jackie returned to Brazil in 1984 to continue mission ministry in some of the same locations and among many of the same people they had served previously—encouraging the young pastors, workers, and Christian families. Twelve years later she retired, but still continues to live a portion of each year in Brazil.

Richard Lee Jr. (Rick), their eldest, went to be with the Lord just 15 years after his father, in September 1996; he left behind his wife, Vikki, and children, Rachel and Ryan; Rachel is now married to Matt Brown and they have a daughter, Victoria.

T. Edward (Ted), their second son is an attorney in Plymouth, Indiana. He and his wife Brenda, still live in Argos. They have two adult children, Phillip and Tracy; both are graduates of Bethel College, Mishawaka, Indiana.

C. Anita, their only daughter—still happy that she was born in Brazil—has an international family of own now. She married Roger Riquelme from Chile; they have a son, Ricardo who was born in the U.S., and twins Miguel and Michelle, born in Paraguay. They are serving as missionaries in Paraguay.

Michael Lynn, their youngest son, married Joanne Clark—an MK (missionary kid)—from Jamaica. They served under World Partners of the Missionary Church for 10 years: eight of these years, in Spain. Their children are Alexis, Jeremy, and Madelyn Joy.

* * *

"We have survived and are all serving the Lord. However, there are moments when we would feel so good if we could have that Special Loved One near us all. What a great encouragement to have in our hearts the anticipation of that marvelous Reunion in Glory. Praise the Lord."

Jackie

Printed in the United States
81722LV00004B/124-348